"Over the course of nineteen years of 24/7 worship and prayer, I have spent literally thousands of hours with these worship leaders. Time and time again they have escorted me into the Lord's tender presence and washed me with the water of His Word. The treasures found in this devotional come from hearts saturated from unceasing adoration and perpetual prayer."

—Allen Hood, Associate Director, IHOPKC

"Leonard Ravenhill once said that a message born in the mind will only reach the mind, but a message born in the heart will reach the heart. This 40-day devotional was born in the hearts of these authors, and I know it will reach the hearts of a whole generation, leading them into a living encounter with Jesus Christ."

—Corey Russell, author and speaker

"Written by singers and musicians who have lived out the 24/7 prayer reality, this 40-day devotional provides insights that have come from many hours of seeking God in the place of prayer and worship."

—Sean Feucht, founder of Burn 24/7, author, speaker, and worship leader, Bethel Music, Redding, California

"The passion and holy zeal expressed by IHOPKC has been a huge blessing to the prayer and worship movement in Europe. This devotional can help you grow as a worshiping child of God."

—Dr. Johannes Hartl, theologian, author, director of Augsburg House of Prayer, Germany

"I have no doubt you will be blessed by the depth of insight, practical wisdom, and love for Jesus that is found in the pages of this book. I have worked with many of these worship leaders on a daily basis for a decade now, and I can honestly say their walk with the Lord is real and the way it comes out in worship is authentic and beautiful. This devotional will encourage and challenge you."

—Chris Tofilon, songwriter and worship leader

"There's so much to gain from spending the next 40 days in this devotional, as each writer shares treasures they've received during their time in the house of prayer. This is a great tool for starting a fresh dialogue with Jesus!"

—Lesley Phillips, worship leader and songwriter

SATISFY
MY
SOUL

A 40-DAY WORSHIP DEVOTIONAL

BroadStreet

PUBLISHING

BroadStreet Publishing® Group, LLC
Savage, Minnesota, USA
BroadStreetPublishing.com

Satisfy My Soul: A 40-Day Worship Devotional

978-1-4245-5809-4 (faux leather)
978-1-4245-5810-0 (e-book)

Stock or custom editions of BroadStreet Publishing titles may be purchased in bulk for educational, business, ministry, fundraising, or sales promotional use. For information, please email info@broadstreetpublishing.com.

Cover and interior by GarborgDesign.com

Printed in China
19 20 21 22 23 5 4 3 2 1

CONTENTS

During the reign of King David, we read about the establishing of a new full-time occupation—that of Levitical singers and musicians who were freed from other duties so that they could be employed in a new work of day-and-night ministering before the Lord with music and song (1 Chr. 9:33, 16:37; 2 Chr. 8:12–14).

One of my greatest joys over the past twenty years has been to see the Lord again raising up singers and musicians across the earth who have given their lives to this full-time occupation, ministering to the Lord with worship music and prayer. This high calling is a great privilege; it comes with many challenges, yet it is worth it because it is an essential part of God's plan to release a great revival across the nations, which will eventually lead to Jesus' return.

As I read this devotional, I am stirred by the many young people who have given the strength of their years to the Lord as singers and musicians. It has truly been an honor to co-labor with many of those who have written these devotions. I encourage all of our singers and musicians to stay the course, but I too am inspired by the faithfulness of those who lead us in ministering to the Lord 24/7 from the stage in our prayer room. As I think of the love, skill, and dedication of people like Justin Rizzo, Jon Thurlow, Laura Park, Matt Gilman,

Brenton Dowdy, Caleb Edwards, and so many of those included here, I am grateful for what the Lord has done through their daily faithfulness.

One of the key objectives of this devotional is to encourage you to maintain a "burning heart." That is a term used by the disciples who engaged Jesus on the road to Emmaus. The same type of burning heart is available to us as believers today, which happens as God reveals God, setting the heart on fire. The global prayer movement that the Holy Spirit is orchestrating today is established as Jesus, the living Word, opens the written Word to the hearts of His people until the first commandment is established in first place in their lives. That happens in a dynamic way through singing and praying the Word back to Him.

I encourage you not to read this devotional like an ordinary book, but use it in conjunction with your Bible reading and your worship times. As you engage with the Lord, I am confident He will satisfy your soul.

Mike Bickle
Director, International House of Prayer, Kansas City

INTRODUCTION BY
Jono Hall

Isn't praying 24/7 a bit excessive? It's a sentiment we have heard through the years, and it's actually the same accusation that Judas Iscariot had against Mary of Bethany's extravagant anointing of Jesus. You should be doing other things; you should be spending your valuable resources elsewhere. Jesus rebuked this accusation and accepted Mary's offering. The truth is that if there were twenty-five hours in a day and eight days in a week, Jesus would be worth more devotion. There is no limit to the worthiness of Jesus.

That is why I love the mandate of the International House of Prayer in Kansas City. I have been part of this community for fifteen years, but in my early years I was a worship leader like many of the writers in this devotional. As I read through these pages, I can imagine myself in the IHOPKC briefing room before a two-hour prayer meeting, preparing my heart and listening to the exhortation of each of the worship leaders. I want to encourage you as you read this book to do likewise.

What you have in your hand are devotional thoughts from many of the worship leaders who keep the "fire on the altar" burning 24/7. Solomon encouraged us in Proverbs to "Keep your heart with all diligence, For out of it spring the issues of life" (Prov. 4:23). This devotional is aimed at helping you "keep your heart." In reading these devotions from worship leaders at IHOPKC and other friends around the world, you will be given a daily Scripture, an inspirational devotion, a prayer, and some thoughts for reflection or journaling. Take your time with this. I encourage you to read, meditate on the words, and engage your heart with the Lord. You will receive revelation as you do so.

We have also included a few song recommendations with each devotional, and a code at the back of this book to get a three-month subscription to UNCEASING, our growing library of spontaneous worship recorded live at IHOPKC, so that you can engage with the Lord with anointed worship music. Mixing anointed music and prayer is a biblical way to place your heart before the Lord and see Him satisfy your soul. I pray the Lord blesses you on this journey.

Jono Hall
Senior Leadership, IHOPKC

Section 1

The Beauty of the Lord

DAY 1

Connecting with a Person

JON THURLOW

That the God of our Lord Jesus Christ, the Father
of glory, may give to you a spirit of wisdom and of
revelation in the knowledge of Him. I pray that the eyes
of your heart may be enlightened.

EPHESIANS 1:17–18A (NASB)

One of the questions I'm often asked as a worship
leader is, "What keeps you going year after year?
What sustains you?" It's a great question. I basically
do the same exact thing at the International House of
Prayer in Kansas City (IHOPKC) every day. Same songs,
same prayers, and the same Scripture passages. And
trust me, whether they're old songs that I've sung a
hundred times or the latest popular worship chorus, it
can easily all start to feel the same!

But there's at least one thing that is not the same,
and it is what sustains me: connecting with Jesus in
worship. It's one thing to sing a song, even a worship
song that's supposed to be sung *to* Jesus. I've done that

many times. But it's a different thing to connect *with* Jesus through song.

I remember when this began to happen to me in a consistent way. I was in my mid-twenties and had been at IHOPKC maybe a year or two. Mike Bickle, IHOPKC director, was giving a message about engaging with God in prayer. He said that when he prayed, he would picture the brilliant light of the Holy Spirit on the inside, or he would picture God's throne room, as described in Revelation 4. For whatever reason, I really locked into the Revelation 4 idea and began to picture that throne room scene when I would pray during my own devotional time with the Lord.

What I didn't know was that this heart posture in my devotions would spill over into my times of leading worship—and it did. Instead of just singing through worship songs and trying to get the room hyped up, I would dial down on the inside, picture that throne room scene, and picture myself before the Lord in that throne room. When that happened, my worship changed. It went from just singing a song to live interaction with the living God through song.

I'd love to say that since that time it just automatically happens every time I step on stage to lead worship in a corporate setting, but it doesn't. Most times when it happens, I'm intentionally reaching to connect with the Lord. I'm being purposeful. I say no to the different distractions in my mind, and no to coasting through a worship set on autopilot. I reach for that intimate connection and dial down on the inside. With focus, I picture myself in that holy throne room, and I picture the Lord. And it makes all the difference between a sing-along or a holy encounter with Jesus.

Jesus, open the eyes of my heart when I'm speaking or singing to you, and give me grace to connect with you in moments of worship!

What are some ways that you can be intentional about connecting with Jesus in the place of worship?

SONG RECOMMENDATIONS

"Jesus, You're Beautiful" by Jon Thurlow
from *Love Makes Us Strong*

"All that You Are" by Jon Thurlow
from *The Anointed One*

DAY 2

One Thing I've Desired

JUSTIN RIZZO

One thing I have desired of the LORD,
That will I seek:
That I may dwell in the house of the LORD
All the days of my life,
To behold the beauty of the LORD,
And to inquire in His temple.

PSALM 27:4

Since 2004, I've been a full-time worship leader on staff at the International House of Prayer in Kansas City, Missouri (IHOPKC). Full-time staff have a fifty-hour work week. We spend twenty-five hours in service (training, leading worship, admin, teaching, etc.) and twenty-five hours in our prayer room.

You may be thinking what a lot of people think when they hear this. *Wow, I'd love to spend that much time in God's presence.*

Whenever someone says this to me, I kindly nod and agree, but I actually want to say, *You should try it sometime and see how that goes for you!* Sitting in a prayer room for hours a week might sound like a constant blissful experience of God's presence (and sometimes it is). But there are times when it's downright grueling and I want nothing more than to leave the room.

In the thousands of hours I've spent in our prayer room over the years, I've meditated on Psalm 27:4 often. It's been one of my go-to lifelines. Here are some key learnings I have had:

First, consider the source. Psalm 27 was written by King David. David is mentioned more than anyone else in the Bible besides Jesus. He was "the man after God's own heart" from whose lineage Jesus is coming and on whose throne Jesus will reign. The point is, David's not just some random guy in the Bible; he's a big deal. So when I read Psalm 27:4, I take note.

Second, the King of Israel is sharing a secret here. The primary preoccupation of David's heart was to gaze on the Lord's beauty. This was the key to his power through seventy years of consistently walking with God. When successful people share their secrets, we do well to listen.

Third, David is sharing what gripped his heart *all* the days of his life, not just in one season. As a teenager, he gazed on God's beauty while playing his guitar on Bethlehem's hillsides as he tended sheep and sang love songs to God. In his twenties, he looked to God as his refuge as jealous King Saul was chasing him through the hills and caves of Judea trying to kill him. In his thirties, forties, and fifties, he inquired of the Lord as king over Israel, defeating the Lord's enemies in tremendous victories. These words sustained David in every season of life, and they can do the same for us.

Finally, David was uniquely drawn by the grace of God into the subject of God's beauty. He beheld the beauty of God in creation when he looked at the stars (Ps. 148:3), in the written word of God as he had it in that day (Ps. 18:30), and in God's character as he experienced forgiveness and redemption (Ps. 32:1).

If David were to hold a self-help or life motivation seminar, you can guarantee that sitting at the feet of Jesus and gazing upon Him would be atop his list of must do's. Another thing I think he would say, and this one's a kicker: God's beauty is evident in every facet of life if only we will look for it.

Father, I want to learn to gaze on your beauty like David did so that in every season and in every place, you are evident in my life. Be the one thing I am after all the days of my life.

As you go throughout your day today, whether you're feeling dry in a prayer room, sitting at a stoplight, or tending to your children at home, write down key phrases that strike your heart from Psalm 27:4 and whisper them to the Lord throughout the day.

SONG RECOMMENDATIONS

"I'm in Love" by Tim Reimherr
from *Let the Weak Speak*

"Pledge" by Marcus Meier
from *Merchant Band*

DAY 3

Step Outside and See

LAURA HACKETT PARK

For ever since the world was created, people have seen the earth and sky. Through everything God made, they can clearly see his invisible qualities—his eternal power and divine nature. So they have no excuse for not knowing God.

ROMANS 1:20 (NLT)

Most of us spend our days inside on a computer, on our phones, boxed in a room with not many windows, taking long car rides in traffic and breathing in recycled air with fluorescent lights shining down on us. In the monotony of life, we can forget about the outside or even complain about the current weather patterns. While the solace of shelter really is a gift, with the wrong perspective life can turn into a suffocating existence inside a box.

I have spent the majority of my days the last fifteen years in a prayer room in Kansas City. It's been a glorious time of singing the Bible and talking with God. I have developed a rich inner life with the Holy Spirit, but I found myself feeling like I couldn't breathe some days. I felt restless and in need of a distraction. So I'd pick up my phone and scroll through an app. Or I'd feel the need for a snack, even if I had just eaten. It's like my body was signaling that I needed something else. There is a certain exhaustion to life, but I began to feel tired all the time.

Sometimes, in a life of ministry and focus on the Spirit, we can lessen the power of the senses and forget the value of the temporary but very real creation around us. In Romans 1, Paul reminds us that the temporary visible world actually speaks to us of the nature and power of God. It's like we were made to take in the world around us and talk to God about it all! We are called not just to the invisible spiritual things, but to look around, take a breath, enjoy a meal, and listen to the people and sounds that surround us.

I began to feel the Holy Spirit drawing me to stop and feel my own restlessness. What was I really craving? Was it really another fifteen minutes of zoning out on my phone that I needed, or another cup of coffee? I would sing and say all day that I wanted to know God more, but I hadn't realized that I began to believe the world around me wasn't important for my life in God. This is when Scriptures like Psalm 19 and Romans 1 began to change me: "The heavens declare the glory of God" and "He has made His wonderful attributes to be easily perceived."

Step outside and see was the simple invitation I began to hear. Just walking outside, looking up, and taking a deep breath can change your perspective on a day. Living my life with my eyes wide open can be painful at times. To really take in the world around us and see how much beauty we have missed—or how much pain and confusion exist—is difficult to face. But this kind of living has drawn me into the deepest worship and conversations with my Lord.

You cannot stay the same if you step outside and open your eyes. There is too much detail and extravagant, almost wasteful beauty to deny that there must be a creative mind behind it all. There are powerful elements in the delicate balance of shocking coexistence—ocean and land, fire and rain. Who draws borders and sets nations in place? Consider a pregnant woman, growing another small, totally unique human on the inside! The science of the world around us and within us is fascinating and exhilarating if we open our eyes to the wonder it holds.

I found that the more holistically I lived, remembering the natural world around me, the richer my worship and inner life in God became. Authentic worship comes from a responsive heart. I could not worship what I didn't see or hadn't encountered. I first had to witness that God existed and then I could respond. Phrases like "You must be an artist!" and "You are a master craftsman!" began to explode out of me as I simply opened my eyes more and observed. This response of faith then manifested itself through my words, actions, emotions, and life decisions.

This is why encounter and worship are so vitally linked. Jesus explained the glory of the kingdom within us by using parables from the natural world. It's so necessary that in all our study, prayer, and worship times we look up and see the evidential power of His creation in the world around us.

Lord, you made all of creation and said it was "GOOD!" Help me see your goodness here in the land of the living. Open my eyes to see the people and life that is right in front of me today.

What is one practical way you can engage with God and the world around you today? (For me, it's been simply taking time outside every day.)

SONG RECOMMENDATIONS

"Majestic" by Jon Thurlow
from *Psalms: Songs of David*

"See the Way" by Misty Edwards
from *Always on His Mind*

DAY 4

Created for His Pleasure

MATT GILMAN

"You are worthy, O Lord,
To receive glory and honor and power;
For You created all things,
And by Your will they exist and were created."
REVELATION 4:11

When I was twenty-five years old, a close friend of mine asked a question I didn't see coming, and one I didn't really have an answer to at the moment. I panicked at the thought of it. Honestly, I lost sleep over it for weeks.

"What is your dream in life? And how do you aspire to make it happen?"

I started worship leading when I was fourteen years old at a Lutheran church in a small town in South Dakota. I moved to Kansas City when I turned eighteen, immediately after I graduated high school. I pursued a career in leading worship and was given amazing opportunities to lead worship in front of large crowds of people.

But was this really my dream?

I enjoyed what I did. Leading worship was, and still is, my passion. I love singing and watching people passionately pour out their hearts to the Lord in song, tears, dance, repentance, and many other ways. I've gotten to travel all over the world. I've had the privilege of watching different cultures worship Jesus in their own languages and in their own expressions. I truly love what I do. But the platform, in and of itself, doesn't really satisfy me. The influence and the notoriety, though they feel good in the moment, have never really left me content.

I remember leading worship in Houston at Reliant Stadium, home of the Houston Texans football team. There were close to 50,000 people in attendance for a worship and prayer gathering called by the governor of Texas. In the middle of one of my songs, I remember that question popped back into my mind: *What is your dream?*

There I was, living out what many people have dreamt of doing: singing in front of tens of thousands of people in one of the largest arenas in the country. Yet this question continued to haunt me.

I began to think about the words to the songs I was singing. Many of my songs are themed around Revelation chapter 4 and the beautiful throne room scene described in it. We all know the song of the seraphim: "Holy, holy, holy, Lord God Almighty, Who was and is and is to come." But there's another song in that chapter that doesn't usually get as much attention. It's the song of the twenty-four elders that encircle the throne. It says they cast their crowns before the One on the throne, they fall down before Him, and they declare that He is worthy of glory, honor and power. Why? Because He created everything in the first place. And it is by His will and for His pleasure that everything exists and was created.

I want to tell you something today: Your highest calling as a human being is to bring glory to the heart of your Creator. He didn't make you because He needed you. He made you because He desired you. You make Him happy. You make His heart glad. You move Him like nothing else in creation ever possibly could. It doesn't matter what your occupation is, how much money you make, how many friends you have, or how much influence you have. Your calling to simply make Him happy transcends all of that.

At the end of the day when I stand before God, my influence, money, popularity, and singing ability all mean nothing. What truly matters is my heart before Him. Did I truly love Him well? Did I worship Him with all that I am, or was it all to entertain a crowd? If I can be honest with you, the platform in front of multitudes is not where I find my greatest sense of fulfillment. It's fun, but my greatest moments are spent before the Lord, alone in my living room, playing my piano, and singing His Word back to Him.

I finally found my dream. And I'm living it out every day.

Father, reveal to me the true meaning of why you made me. Deliver me from the need to perform and allow me to simply rest in knowing that I was created for your pleasure.

When do you feel the pleasure of God the most? What is something you could do to enjoy Him more each day?

SONG RECOMMENDATIONS

"All Is for Your Glory" by Lisa Gottshall and Laura Hackett Park (sung by Cory Asbury) from *Onething Live: Magnificent Obsession*

"Breathe" by Matt Gilman from *Touching Heaven*

DAY 5

Nothing Too Precious for Jesus

CALEB ANDREWS

"The kingdom of heaven is like treasure hidden in a field, which a man found and covered up. Then in his joy he goes and sells all that he has and buys that field."

MATTHEW 13:44 (ESV)

In 1895, Amy Wilson Carmichael left her homeland of Ireland to serve as a missionary overseas. When she died in 1951, she had spent fifty-five years serving tirelessly without furlough, working for her Lord among the needy in India.

Life was hard in those days and even harder for a missionary serving abroad. Amy never married and was bedridden much of her last twenty-five years on earth.

Her impact on my life has been immense. When I read her story I ask, *Why give so much? Why work so hard? Why love with such abandon?* I think she answers those questions best through her motto: "Nothing is too precious for Jesus." That was the theme of her life, and that is the message of Matthew 13:44. There's a treasure hidden in a field. It's not observable to everyone, but those who discover its value are compelled to sell everything to have it.

I believe Jesus is that treasure. Amy and countless other saints have found that treasure and responded accordingly. But what exactly did they see in this Jewish man that they considered to be a "treasure"? Was it His patience? His power? His willingness to lay down His life for mankind? Yes, and so much more.

The reasons why Jesus is and forever will be worthy of our worship and obedience are endless. When the eyes of our heart finally behold this truth, we too will say, "Nothing is too precious for Jesus." The danger we face in the twenty-first century is to be blinded by the many so-called "treasures" reaching for our attention. If we are not careful, we will wind up investing our life's energy in things that are not worthy and sell all we have to buy a field with no treasure in it. If we make such a terrible mistake, we will find ourselves greatly ashamed when we at last see the treasure of all treasures.

I struggle along like the rest of us to daily push aside the entanglements of this age. Even in ministry, we can so easily be absorbed with ourselves and our aspirations that we wind up losing vision of the worth of our Lord. It should not be.

The aim of Christianity is not to put on display the worth of this world, but to put on display the worth of Jesus. This should be the aim of our preaching, relationships, worship, and work. His beauty and worth will carry us into a way of life that is in total contrast to the world around us. He is altogether lovely and oh how much He has given for us. May God enable us today to see the worth of Jesus and live in a way that proves it to those around us.

Father, enable us to see the worth of your Son.
Turn our eyes from worthless things
and give us the Spirit of wisdom and revelation.

What earthly "treasures" are pulling your gaze from the worth of Jesus? How can you reset your gaze on that which is truly worthy?

SONG RECOMMENDATIONS

"Come Now Joy" by Justin Rizzo
from *Fully Alive*

"No Other Name" by Laura Hackett Park
from *Onething Live: All Cry Glory*

DAY 6

Your Face Is Lovely

NAOMI RIZZO

My dove in the clefts of the rock,
in the hiding places on the mountainside,
show me your face,
let me hear your voice;
for your voice is sweet,
and your face is lovely.

SONG OF SOLOMON 2:14 (NIV)

Do you ever cry when you go to the movies? I have never been the type to burst into tears in the theater, but I did at *Princess Diaries 2*. In one scene, Princess Mia is in an Independence Day parade, waving at people lining the streets. When the princess sees some boys teasing a little girl, she stops the entire parade to help. Upon learning she and her friends are orphans, she gives them all tiaras and invites them to join the parade. Instantly tears began to stream down my face. Before my mind could understand what was going on, my emotions displayed a heartfelt response of something deeper.

I was moved because that little girl represented me. In the same way the princess reaches out to comfort this little girl, God was showing me that He stops everything to bend down and lift me up to where He is. God stopped me that day and said, *Come join me in this Freedom Day parade. Let me love you where you're at.*

Song of Solomon 2:14 has spoken to my heart so many times over the years. God calls me "lovely and beautiful" even though the reality is so many times the complete opposite when I feel broken, messed up, and weak. It's in that place of brokenness that the majestic, high, and Holy One declares, *Your voice is sweet and your face is lovely.* Life suddenly comes into divine perspective when He speaks these words.

Here's a truth easy to forget: God is not seeking the strong. He came for the weak— you and me. He wants our honesty. He wants us to voice our disappointments, perplexities, and pains to Him. He wants to break down your facade of strength you would try and demonstrate to Him and fill you with His perfect love.

No matter what others have or haven't spoken over your life, He is the great validator and His words go deeper than anyone else's. He wants you to know His validation as your Father so that you won't look for others to fill that place.

He's the closest friend, ready to hear your cry for help and respond. He positions Himself wherever you need Him and whenever you cry out. In your weakness He is there, ready to be strong on your behalf. He bends down to tend and cultivate the beautiful flower of your heart to make sure it blooms and grows.

How do we tap into that well? Many times, it's as simple as turning your attention—stopping during the day and taking a few moments to recognize His presence in your life. As we bare our souls in honesty before Him, the river of life flows.

You are hidden in your Father who delights in you and has unending desire for relationship with you. His voice is calling to you: *Let me hear your voice, let me see your face, because your face is lovely, and your voice is sweet.* When you spend time with Him, your old self dies and your mind is renewed.

Jesus, your voice is the one I want to hear clearly in my life. I ask that my ears would be opened to your voice and all other noise would stop today. Let me hear you declaring over me that you genuinely love who I am.

Pause today and take a moment to ask God to stop the parade and turn His attention upon you. As you experience His presence, ask Him a simple question: "What do you think about me?" Write down what you hear.

SONG RECOMMENDATIONS

"Dark but Lovely" by Sarah Edwards
from *Constant*

"You've Set Me Free" by Justin Rizzo
from *Shout Your Name*

DAY 7

Your Emojis
Always Matter

CALEB EDWARDS

Therefore, since we have a great high priest who has
passed through the heavens—Jesus the Son of God—let
us hold fast to our confession. ... let us approach the
throne of grace with boldness, so that we may receive
mercy and find grace to help us in time of need.

HEBREWS 4:14, 16 (CSB)

Take just a moment and speak out the simple
words, "I love you, Jesus." Now, imagine those
words leaving your mouth. If you are more visual or
imaginative like me, maybe picture those words as the
heart emoji. Like a helium balloon, watch that little emoji
as it floats high into the sky until it is completely out of
sight. Picture it unstoppable as it passes through the
clouds and into the cosmos. Eventually, your little "I
love Jesus" emoji passes into the halls of heaven, and
into the throne room of God where it falls into a golden
bowl of incense and is transformed into a fragrant waft

of smoke. That waft of smoke begins its flowing journey toward the center of that room, where eventually the Man who is God, King Jesus, breathes it in through His very real nose.

Each time we pray, this is the journey of our weak words. Each time we sing that chorus of tender adoration from our place of desperation, there is a holy inhalation. Nothing has transformed my understanding of worship more than this simple revelation: Jesus is human. The transformation of our song and speech into a fragrant incense ensures us that our words aren't wasted. Jesus has passed through the heavens, and because of that, He says we can come boldly before the very same throne where He is seated at the right hand of the Father. We are left in a quandary if we take that to mean we can physically go there...maybe one day, but certainly not today. So how do I come boldly? With prayers and songs. Our words travel the distance of earth to heaven and are received as a bold fragrance. A fragrance of incense.

In the fall of 2015, I was leading a small group prayer time with one of our internships here at IHOPKC. I had been excessively busy, and that particular week I came completely unprepared. I just told everyone to close their eyes, honestly hoping that when they did some divine instructions of what was coming next would drop out of the ceiling into my lap. Instead, I sensed one short phrase deep in my inner man: "Talk to me like I am human."

What followed was one of the sweetest, most sincere, most powerful and impactful times of prayer I have experienced. It was in this moment I first imagined Jesus "breathing in my words." It was slightly funny, yet massively transformative to my worship and prayer life. My lack of preparation that day (which I do not recommend) was trumped by the love of a real man on a real throne who truly does desire communion and conversation with me.

I know you may feel a bit disconnected from God at times. We all do. When you feel that way, be reminded that your weak words—whether you feel it or not—are right now in the very air of heaven. God Himself is surrounded by the fragrance of your worship. What an honor! Open your mouth and sing confidently, speak boldly, and worship unhindered. Your words (and your emojis) never hit the ceiling.

Jesus, I love you. Help me to truly trust that you are receiving this simple prayer.

What words do you want to speak to Jesus right now, knowing that He is listening?

SONG RECOMMENDATIONS

"The Man Who Is God" EP by Caleb Edwards

"The Beauty of This Man" by Tim Reimherr
from the IHOPKC collaborative album *Immersed*

DAY 8

Well Pleased

JUSTIN RIZZO

And a voice from heaven said, "This is my Son,
whom I love; with him I am well pleased."

MATTHEW 3:17 (NIV)

My personality is Type A to the max. I'm a content-
producing entrepreneurial builder who's always
got more than a few irons in the fire. I don't purposely
pursue busyness, but I tend to find myself busy a lot.
And I love it.

The other day, I went to a local coffee shop and
spent seven hours working on a project. Now, this
wasn't a half-hearted seven hours; I was engaged. I
had my hoodie up, shielding my eyes from everyone
and everything so the only things I could see were my
fingers typing and the cursor blinking on my screen. I
had my headphones pumping the Gladiator soundtrack
at the perfect volume to cut out all the outside noise.

I was incredibly productive that day.

However, when I was packing up to leave, I began
to get this sinking feeling in my stomach. I was heading

home for family time with my wife and kids when I started feeling like a failure, like I hadn't done enough. Immediately and without realizing it, I began strategizing about how right after I put my kids to bed that night, I could sneak upstairs to my office and do another three or four hours of work before bed.

Surely, I thought, that would make this feeling in my stomach go away. I just needed to be a little more productive that day.

You probably already figured it out, but cramming more hours of work into an already busy day was not the answer. As I drove home, I began asking the Lord how I could do seven hours of uninterrupted work and still feel like a failure. I heard a still, small voice speak one word to me.

Identity.

Only when our identity is found in Him will we experience the pleasures of knowing Him. We were made to enjoy God, not to feel condemned because we aren't doing enough for Him. My daughter doesn't have to do anything to make me feel incredibly proud of her. She can just be.

I love that when Jesus came up from the Jordan after being baptized, the Father declared, "This is my Son, whom I love; with him I am well pleased" (Matt. 3:17 NIV). Jesus hadn't done one miracle or preached one sermon, and from an earthly perspective, He hadn't accomplished anything for God. Yet the Father was pleased.

My problem that day was not with my effort or my

productivity. My problem was that my identity was not resting securely in God's love. Paul knew the importance of finding our identity in the Lord. He prayed that the Ephesians would be strengthened in their inner man by being rooted and grounded in love (Eph. 3:17-19).

I was created to love God and be loved by Him. All the work I do cannot be an attempt to earn God's pleasure; my ministry needs to flow from the knowledge that I already have it.

Lord, help me to see that you are pleased with me before I accomplish or do anything for you. Help my identity to be rooted and grounded in your love, so I can experience the fullness of joy that is found in your presence and feel your pleasures forevermore.

Do you feel like you are disappointing God by not doing enough for Him? Take a moment right now to ask Him how He feels when He looks at you.

SONG RECOMMENDATIONS

"Good, Good Father" by Pat Barrett and Tony Brown
from *Housefires II*

"Come as Close as You Want" by Tim Reimherr
from *The World Can Wait*

DAY 9

Beholding and Becoming

EMI SOUSA

> So all of us who have had that veil removed can see
> and reflect the glory of the Lord. And the Lord—who is
> the Spirit—makes us more and more like him as we are
> changed into his glorious image.
>
> 2 CORINTHIANS 3:18 (NLT)

Several years ago, I found myself going through a
season of mistreatment for the first time in my adult
life. People I respected and trusted in leadership turned
against me and suddenly all I had built in ministry
with them was called into question and began to fall
apart. Lies were being said about my character and
for a moment I found myself alone and disciplined for
something I had not done.

One morning during this season, as I sat alone with
the Bible open in my room, I began to weep over the
pain and confusion I was experiencing. My little brother,
who was two years old at the time, walked in and
climbed into my lap. He looked into my eyes, laid his
hand on my face, and began to cry with me. The more

I cried, the more he cried. I could not understand what was happening between us. Somehow I knew the Lord was there with me, speaking through this beautiful, holy moment with a child, and I began to feel the love of the Father closer than I'd ever felt before.

Suddenly I heard the Lord whisper to me, *You either embrace meekness through this mistreatment or you will walk away offended. Choose to behold my meekness and let it have its way in you.* With clarity, I understood that these circumstances I was walking through were an invitation from the Lord to behold and become more like Him. Would I defend myself or would I look to my defender? The choice was mine. In seasons of great pain, suffering, or mistreatment, we can choose to dwell on the injustice of what is happening to us or we can look to Jesus. It's not a choice we make once, but every day. We are sons and daughters of God, but we will not fully know who we are until we see Jesus. Until then, we are on a journey of transformation.

Do you want to be holy? Then behold Him who is holy. Do you want to love more? Then behold the One who is love. Are you in a season when you need to be more patient? Behold Him who is patient with you. Do you feel you're not as gentle and humble as you want to be? Then behold the One who said, "Learn from me, for I am gentle and humble in heart" (Mt. 11:29 NIV). All Christians can experience transformation daily as they behold the glory of God revealed in His Word, and especially through the One who *is* the Word—the man, Christ Jesus.

Paul writes in 2 Corinthians 3:18, "But we all, with unveiled face, beholding as in a mirror the glory of the Lord, are being transformed into the same image from glory to glory."

We see the image of God through the mirror of God's Word, and as we meditate upon the Word, we experience a gradual transformation. As we observe Christ's glory, we advance in Christlikeness and reflect His glory in our character. This glory will not fade away but will increase over time "from glory to glory," providing we continue to behold the Lord. As I look back on my own story, I can see areas where I have changed. I have been transformed.

As you say *yes* to the transforming work of the Holy Spirit in your life each day, the Word will come alive and you will begin to respond as Jesus would respond. I remember meditating on the Gospels often during that difficult season. Jesus' meek response to His mistreatment suddenly meant more to me. As He hung on the cross, having been crucified by His own people, all He said was, "They do not know what they do" (Luke 23:34). Jesus' words gave me strategies for dealing with the accusations coming against me and helped me get through my pain.

I can say that I walked away from that season unoffended. I began to pray for those who had hurt me. The Word produced compassion in me that I never had. Love that suffers long grew in me. I look back at that season with gratitude and wouldn't trade it for anything. Today, I see what the Holy Spirit produced in me through beholding Christ, which I will carry with me for all eternity.

Jesus, whatever season I'm in, I want to experience personal transformation as I behold the true image of God in your Word. Strengthen me to make right choices and give me grace to react rightly in situations where I am under pressure.

What area in your life do you want to see transformation and growth through beholding Christ?

SONG RECOMMENDATIONS

"Renova a Minha Mente" by Emilaine Sousa
from *Nossa Adoração*

"Quebra o Silêncio" by Emilaine Sousa
from *Grandes Feitos*

"Wounded One" by Davy Flowers
from *Onething Live: Magnificent Obsession*

"I Have Decided" by Jaye Thomas
from *Fully Alive*

DAY 10

Around the Throne

MATT GILMAN

The four living creatures, each having six wings,
were full of eyes around and within.
And they do not rest day or night, saying:
"Holy, holy, holy,
Lord God Almighty,
Who was and is and is to come!"

REVELATION 4:8

I was about to lead worship for a prayer set in the
IHOPKC prayer room as I had done hundreds of times
before. Our focus for the afternoon was on the beauty of
God as described in Revelation 4. I had been fascinated
with this chapter for years. But I remember being so
frustrated with the fact that there are these four living
creatures gathered around His throne right now, and that
they get to see His beauty every moment of every day,
and they sing their songs with such great understanding
of who He is and what He looks like, yet I'm stuck here
on Earth completely separated from it. It seemed unfair
to me, and honestly quite cruel, that God would give

us such a captivating description of what He's like, and then force us to live separated from Him. All of this while at the same time knowing that there are multitudes beholding His glory in eternity in that very moment.

But the Holy Spirit whispered something to me that day, something that changed the way I worship and read the Bible. He said, "You don't have to wait till you get there. You're invited to join in right now." Did you know that through the Word of God and by the escort of the Holy Spirit, you get to experience and participate in what is happening around the throne?

You were created to see God. The reason you have eyes is not so that you can be temporarily entertained by worldly things in this life until you get to behold Him in the next. Your eyes were made for the glory of God... right now! The seraphim in Revelation 4 are covered with eyes all around, and from the moment they were created they have done nothing but gaze upon eternal beauty. Jesus said in the Sermon on the Mount that the lamp of the body is the eye. "If therefore your eye is good, your whole body will be full of light" (Matt. 6:22). What must be happening in the hearts of the seraphim as they look continually at such a matchless and beautiful God?

Jasper. Sardius. Emerald rainbow. Lightnings. Thunderings. Voices. A sea of glass. Seven torches. These four creatures are taking it all in. And when it comes time for them to respond to what they're seeing, the only words that come into their minds to describe

His splendor are, "Holy, holy, holy." Over and over and over they sing it as if it were the first time they'd ever seen Him. "Holy, holy, holy!" For thousands and thousands of years, they've been singing the same song. And by the revelation of the Holy Spirit, you are invited to join in with them.

You were created to be completely captivated and overtaken by Him. Take time today to meditate on the beauty of God. And respond to it by participating in the anthem of heaven around the throne. Lord, you are HOLY!

Father, I want to see you. Open the eyes of my heart to behold the beauty of who you are. I join with heaven right now and say that you are unlike any other. You are holy.

What aspect of God's beauty do you want to behold?

SONG RECOMMENDATIONS

"Holy" by Matt Gilman
from *Awaken Love*

"Storm All Around You" by Jon Thurlow
from *Onething Live: Magnificent Obsession*

Section 2

The Language
of Worship

Let Me Hear Your Voice

LAURA HACKETT PARK

And his voice thundered like mighty ocean waves.
REVELATION 1:15B (NLT)

Then I heard again what sounded like the shout
of a vast crowd or the roar of mighty ocean waves
or the crash of loud thunder.
REVELATION 19:6A (NLT)

Have you ever felt like your voice didn't matter? As if no one was going to listen no matter what you said and you couldn't change anything anyway by speaking up? We live in a time where there is such a deluge of sound hitting the airways. There are so many platforms for opinions and individual expression that adding to the cacophony can feel pointless at times.

I have felt this as a musician and songwriter. Should I get my songs out when the music industry is already flooded with so many new songs and talent? I believe the debilitating feeling that no one is listening is a universal one that living in our generation has exacerbated.

In the book of Revelation, Jesus' resurrected voice is described as the sound of mighty ocean waves (Rev. 1:25). The sound of many waters fills the full sound spectrum and hits the human ear (and beyond). Rushing water has all the high, mid, and low waves that make up the sound spectrum. This simple acoustic data is deeply symbolic to me. The voice of Jesus is full, powerful, and complete, lacking nothing. His sound can reach every creature in all of heaven and earth. Our bodies still reverberate with the energy of His sound that spoke us into being.

With so much power at His disposal it is a wonder that He can "bend His ear" to listen to an individual. "This poor man cried out, and the Lord heard him ..." (Ps. 34:6). What?! God will listen to the voice of one individual out of billions of people! Scripture tells us that He not only hears, but also *wants* to listen to His beloved people.

One of the most life-impacting verses for me is Song of Solomon 2:14, where the Beloved God says, "Let Me hear your voice.... For your voice is sweet [to Me]." He wants to listen to the sound of us talking, singing, and pouring out our hearts to Him. Doesn't this make you want to talk and sing to Him more? The most important Person in the whole world not only listens to you but also cares to hear your thoughts and perspective. This is profoundly encouraging as an individual, but let's take it even a step further.

Revelation 19 tells us that the church will be like a bride who is prepared and ready to be joined to her bridegroom, Jesus. In a verse that can easily be passed over, the voice of the collective church is described as the "roar of mighty ocean waves" (Rev. 19:6 NLT). That's the exact same description of Jesus' voice in Revelation 1. The worldwide bride will be voicing a sound that matches the power and fullness of the Lord's voice. We will be made perfect and complete, lacking nothing together. This means our individual voices matter to Jesus personally and also our unique sound added to the collective voice of the church matters to Him! Talk about a heavenly encouragement to sing together during a worship service.

We are one body, one church, and one bride. When the fullness of the voices from every nation, tribe, and tongue begin to sound, then we will know that it is time to be joined to our Bridegroom, Jesus.

Lord, thank you for listening and valuing the sound of my voice. Help me not to be silent but to talk with you every day.

Describe a time you felt silenced or like your voice didn't matter. How did you respond, and how could you have responded differently?

SONG RECOMMENDATIONS

"King Jesus" by Laura Hackett Park
from *Love Will Have Its Day*

"Beautiful Heart" by Laura Hackett Park
from *Love Will Have Its Day*

DAY 12

Entering with Intent

KENDRIAN DUECK

But when the people come in through the north
gateway to worship the Lord during the religious
festivals, they must leave by the south gateway. And
those who entered through the south gateway must
leave by the north gateway. They must never leave by
the same gateway they came in, but must always use
the opposite gateway.

EZEKIEL 46:9 (NLT)

As we sat on the steps leading up to the Temple Mount,
our guide began to share to our group about the
history of the ancient facade that stood before us. Massive
Herodian-era stone blocks mixed in with replicated
stone make up the steps and walls of the ancient city of
Jerusalem. As we observed the city, our eyes were drawn
to the sheer size and the intricate detail. As we listened,
our guide began to not only share about the historic
architecture, but also the spiritual significance of what was
before us. This is what impacted my heart the most.

Every step and every doorway to us is usually just a
means of getting from where we are to where we need

to be. With technology, we find the fastest and most efficient ways of getting from here to there. Builders typically build around concepts such as efficiency and aesthetic. But here, along the southern wall of the ancient Temple Mount, I saw something else. Every stone laid with intent—every block, every corner, every curve, every chisel mark, placed with purpose and precision, yielding not only physical implications, but spiritual ones. Steps laid at different heights, a shallow step followed by one with a higher rise, completely random with no noticeable pattern. Our guide went on to explain the reasoning behind such oddly laid steps to be nothing other than a means to slow the traveler down and create an entryway of intentionality.

The worshiper traveling up to the Temple Mount is forced to slow down and enter through the gate not in haste and busyness, but at peace and with a reverent heart. The guide then read to us Ezekiel 46:9 and explained the profound and weighty statement made simply by the location of the gates leading into and out of the Temple Mount.

This verse appears to be nothing more than pedestrian traffic laws, but as we begin to read within the context of both the chapter in Ezekiel and the magnitude of what was taking place upon the Mount, our eyes begin to open and we see the heart of God.

As I sat there, I imagined myself walking up those steps, up toward the Holy of Holies and then out again on the other side. Looking past the physical construction, I could now see the heart behind the design. In the same way, through all the religious practice and tradition, I could see the relational heart of the Father. A Father whose heart is not only so deeply moved by us, but also longing for our hearts to be moved in the same way by His love and His nature.

Does my heart walk into worship with intention? Do I slow down enough to catch the new thing that the Lord wants to do in my heart? Do I leave the same way I came and the same person I was when I entered into a church service or moments of prayer? And if so, am I okay with that? I sat provoked. The Lord had laid this on my heart a couple of years prior, but as I looked at the steps, saw the gates, and read that verse for the first time with new perspective, it was as if the Lord was stamping something on my heart—a passion to never put the Lord in a box, to never limit the way He wants to move, or the words He may speak.

God is eternal and infinite, and to Him there is no end. He doesn't have to come but He does, and each and every time we step into worship, the Living God is around us—moving, speaking, whispering, and singing over us. His Presence changes us to look more like Him as we spend time gazing on His face and surrendering our hearts to Him.

Father, give me grace to slow down and spend time
with you intentionally, making you a priority again.
Lord, I want to be continually transformed by your
Holy Spirit and by your Word, each and every time
I meet with you.

**What intentional things can you do the next time you
enter into worship to be able to connect with God and
go deeper in your walk with Him?**

SONG RECOMMENDATIONS

"More" by Jeremy Riddle
from *More*

"Clean Hands" by Lauren Alexandria
from *Victorious in Love*

DAY 13

Giving Him Our Best

BY JON THURLOW

Sing the glory of his name; Make his praise glorious.
PSALM 66:2 (NASB)

In our culture we spend a lot of time and energy making music the best it can be. Classical musicians pour hours and hours into practicing their instruments. Pop stars record their vocals over and over to get just the right sound. Producers go late into the night at their workstations, piecing everything together to make it perfect.

When I think about it, so much of the music created today is void of eternal value. It makes me grateful for our songs of worship—music that will carry into the next age. The fact that we have an opportunity to create music to sing to Jesus on this side of eternity is stunning to me. What a gift and privilege! But then I wonder if we put the same amount of effort and energy into our worship music that the rest of the world puts into theirs? Isn't Jesus worthy of the best we can give?

In my early teens, I decided I wanted to pursue

music as a vocation. I'd been studying piano lessons for a few years but began to approach music in a more serious way. More hours of practice, more competitions, more study. I didn't want to become a classical virtuoso, but I wanted the tools that the training offered because I had a vision to do music with excellence.

When I think of musical excellence in worship, I think of skill, emotion, and heart position.

To develop the skill of singing or playing an instrument requires technical learning and practice, just like any craft. As worship leaders, singers, and musicians, have we taken the time to study? Have we taken voice or instrument lessons? To me, the goal isn't to become technically perfect, but rather to have the tools needed for creating music that is beautiful.

What about emotion? Music isn't just technique, but also an art—and art is all about expression. Do we put feeling, expression, and emotion into our music? It's a huge part of helping the worshiper connect! When I'm recruiting musicians for my worship band, I look for a measure of technical skill, but I'm looking even more for depth of feeling and emotion. Does the musician "feel" the music when he or she plays? Do they pour passion into it? Can they pick up on the emotional mood that I'm creating, and play off of it?

Ultimately, excellence in worship is about heart position. Most songs in the world are about telling a story. But when we talk about worship music, we're talking about singing to someone. And that begs the question, "How well do we know the person we're singing to?" Have we cultivated a history with the Lord? Do we consistently spend time in His Word, in the place of prayer, connecting with His heart? If we only connect with the Lord when we're onstage, how real is that connection? People can sense authentic worship, and authentic worship happens when we have a vibrant life in God.

As I write, I feel convicted. I've pursued excellence in a measure, but I'm aware that I need to say "yes" again in certain areas. What about you? Do you have a vision for excellence in worship? Are you committed to giving Jesus your best?

When I graduated from college, I was a backslidden Christian but wanted to change. When I heard about the house of prayer in Kansas City, I decided to do a three-month internship. After doing the internship and joining the staff, it was still over a year before my heart started coming alive in God again. There were a handful of gifted worship leaders, singers, and musicians on staff at the time who were offering Jesus their best in worship—and the Lord used them to help sustain me that first year. I thought, *If people this gifted are giving the prayer room thing a shot, maybe I should stick around.* That was fourteen years ago now, and I'm so thankful for how God used them to help keep me steady!

In this hour of history, I believe God is raising up young singers and musicians who are willing to give Him their best, who are committed to making His praise glorious. They will impact and inspire their generation, and ultimately will testify of the inestimable worth of Jesus.

Jesus, give me a vision for excellence in worship, and help me as I aim to give you my best.

What are some practical things you can be doing in this season to grow as a singer or musician, both skill-wise and heart-wise?

SONG RECOMMENDATIONS:

"Worthy of It All" by David Brymer
from *Onething Live: Magnificent Obsession*

"All That's Inside" by Jon Thurlow
from *Strong Love*

DAY 14

Drawing Near in Brokenness

MICHAEL & BECCI BALL

The righteous cry out, and the LORD hears,
And delivers them out of all their troubles.
The LORD is near to those who have a broken heart,
And saves such as have a contrite spirit.

PSALM 34:17–18

Recently, in a single day, we received three separate pieces of news that impacted our ministry, our finances, and our family life. In just one day, we went from feeling secure and full of purpose to suddenly needing to rethink almost every area of our lives. Sometimes life is hard and it feels like everything is going against you. It can feel like the plans and promises of God are just so far off. In fact, in the days and weeks after that news, we questioned if God was even with us. We were tired, frustrated, discouraged, and angry. We were broken.

We learned a valuable lesson because of that day.

It turns out this is not a subject that God has ever been silent about. His Word is *full* of promises for us to believe and appropriate. They remind us of who He is—we can stand on them and declare their truth in every situation. The Bible tells us that while we will face trials (1 Peter 1:6–9), and while we will face opposition (Phil. 1:27–28), He is with us right in the midst of it (Ps. 23:5), not waiting for us to get things back together, but preparing a table for us to sit with Him, drink, and be anointed again by Him.

Our best response to brokenness is to pray. When we invite Him into our brokenness, He responds (Matt. 5:4). We don't need to be "on the mend," we don't need to be eloquent, and we don't even need to see a light at the end of the tunnel. We simply need to call out to Him, share our broken heart with Him, and allow Him to begin to speak to us and heal our hearts (Matt. 11:28–30).

For us, we began an intense season of songwriting where, in spite of our situation, we were able to sing His word and His promises over our lives and watch as He mercifully began piecing our hearts back together. As we soaked ourselves in His Word and shared our disappointments and pain with Him, He showed us how He had always been with us and how much He loved us, and He gradually lifted our eyes and restored our hope. All the confusion and doubt began to pale into insignificance at the grace and the mercy and the greatness of our God. The songs that came out of that season are a constant reminder both of that difficult season, but also His deliverance.

When you feel overwhelmed and brokenhearted, we want to encourage you that His heart for you hasn't changed. His passionate love for you hasn't diminished. If you will call out to Him, He will draw near to you. Remember, He fully understands what it's like to be human (Heb. 4:15) and heartbroken, so we should boldly and confidently come before Him and allow Him to begin to heal our hearts and work in our lives. If you give it to Him, He will meet you and begin to restore you.

Lord, I thank you that in every season of my life, you are with me, you are for me and you are good. Today I open my heart to you fully. I give to you all pain, disappointment, hurt, and rejection, and I ask you to heal my heart.

What area of your heart do you need God to heal today?

SONG RECOMMENDATIONS:

"In Every Season" by Michael & Becci Ball
from *Holy One*

"Leaning" by Justin Rizzo
from *Onething Live: All Cry Glory*

DAY 15

Fill Your Mouth with Praise

LUKE WOOD

I will bless the Lord at all times;
His praise shall continually be in my mouth.
PSALM 34:1

Why is music such an integral part of the human experience? There is no doubt that humans are musical creatures. There is something ingrained in us—even as children—that says music will be an important part of our human experience. A mother sings a lullaby to her baby as he falls asleep. In grade school, children memorize facts and details by singing a simple melody. As we grow older through adolescence and into adulthood, certain songs bring comfort through the trials of life and impact us profoundly. We are moved by music not because of any flaw caused by sin, but because God is the author of music. He enjoys music, and we are made in His image. We were created with the capacity to enjoy, express, and connect through music.

As we journey through life, time has a tendency to weather our hearts. Time can beat down even the strongest resolve in us, producing pain and wounds that never heal. The way that we process pain is of crucial importance. Tough circumstances present themselves to each of us, and it's how we choose to deal with these difficulties that ultimately shows who we are. At the end of the day, how you respond to pain reveals everything about your character.

It is no coincidence that about 70 percent of the psalms are laments. Humanity can't ignore or avoid pain. For David, the circumstances in his life that produced suffering were his escort into prayerful dialogue with the Lord. David faced disappointment, suffering, and pain head on and turned it into prayerful song. Pain was his escort into a real and authentic conversation. Suffering doesn't always make us better people; in fact, it can do just the opposite. Pain can produce wounds that, if not dealt with, lead to bitterness and offense.

David failed as a father, husband, leader, and spiritual person. The life of David is not a story about a man who never failed, but it *is* the story of a man who remained penitent and refused to give up. When David was in trouble, when he was scared and unsure, he sang his prayers to the one who could hear and the one who would answer.

I recently had a health scare. I didn't know what the future held for me as I awaited the official diagnosis. The thought of my wife and children growing up without a husband and father was almost more than I could bear. For several long days, I had nothing but long hours to wrestle with the thought that my time on earth could be limited. I remember sitting down with my guitar and singing raw and broken words to the Lord as I voiced my concerns, questions, and fears. The Holy Spirit flooded my heart in that moment and I knew that He was with me. The diagnosis finally came back and everything turned out all right in the end, but I will never forget singing those prayers in my hour of trouble and finding the Lord present with me.

I believe God places something melodic in each of us as children that whispers to our hearts as we grow up. We were made to sing. Music is able to direct and steer our thoughts and emotions toward the Lord. It is no wonder that Paul taught his early church communities to sing and make melody as they grew in the faith.

Offering authentic worship in the midst of a difficult circumstance moves the heart of God. Singing truth even through disappointment is one of the healthiest ways to process the pain and challenges life can bring. Fill your mouth with praise.

Lord, give me a heart like David to sing in every situation. Anchor me in the truth that you delight in me. Let your praise always be on my lips.

What do you want to express to God right now? Write down what is in your heart—no matter what it is—and turn it into a song.

SONG RECOMMENDATIONS

"Pour Out Mercy" by Luke Wood
from *The Law and the Prophets*

"Kiss My Soul" by Luke Wood
from *The Law and the Prophets*

DAY 16

Songs from the Valley

MATT GILMAN

Yea, though I walk through the valley
of the shadow of death,
I will fear no evil;
For You are with me;
Your rod and Your staff, they comfort me.

PSALM 23:4

I want a divorce. Four of the most heart-wrenching words you can ever hear from your spouse. Words that, unfortunately, are all too familiar in Christian marriages. Words that even I had to hear. It was a journey I was not prepared for. And in my thirty-three years on this earth, it was the darkest and most difficult time in my life. I had so many questions. For her. For God. What would I do? Who could I turn to? But in the midst of all of my fears and anxieties, and as I used every ounce of emotional strength I had in me to put one foot in front of the other to walk this excruciating path, I heard His still, small voice whisper to me: *Sing ... just sing.* With every single step, I heard Him reminding me to *just sing*.

As a worship leader in full-time ministry, I felt disqualified. My marriage had failed, so I labeled myself a failure as a husband. A failure as a father. And ultimately, a failure before God. I didn't know what my life would look like moving forward. Everything seemed so dark and all I could feel was immense shame. But I still couldn't get His voice out of my head reminding me to lift up my song. When the shadow in the valley was dark, He was faithful to speak to me and tell me to just love Him in the midst of my brokenness. It was then that I realized I had a choice to make: I could choose to become angry, hold a grudge, and harbor bitterness in my heart, or I could choose to love and worship Him through my pain.

Psalm 34 says to "bless the Lord at all times." It's easy to take that verse and apply it in seasons of joy and success. But it's a whole different story to apply it in seasons of pain and discomfort. Sometimes singing feels like the last thing I want to do. Sometimes it's easy to be angry with God or with people. When you're surrounded by darkness, there is so much that is unknown, so much you can't see. The darkness creates unwarranted fear in your heart. It creates doubt that He's with you, by your side, and there to comfort you.

Oh, but let me encourage you today. He promised that He would never leave you or forsake you. He promised that He would be your light when the pangs of death and darkness surround you. There is no reason to be afraid of the unknown because He is still sovereign over the unknown. He sees your end from your beginning. Nothing takes Him by surprise. And there is something about worshiping and being vulnerable before Him when you're in the darkest valley that moves His heart in such a unique way. I promise you, He will see you through whatever season you're in, good or bad.

Whether you're enjoying the success of your greatest victory, or you're struggling in the depths of your deepest valley ... sing. Just sing. If you don't think you have a good voice, just sing anyway. If you've never been given a microphone to sing on a platform, just sing. Go to the secret place, and sing out your joy, sing your songs of rejoicing, sing out your pain, sing your songs of lament. He's for you. He's with you. And He will lead you through your circumstances with grace and perfection.

Father, thank you for your leadership. Reveal your kindness to me in a deeper way, and remind me that you're constantly with me and on my side, no matter my circumstance.

What area of your life do you need to sing over today? Freewrite lyrics of praise or pain, and then sing them.

SONG RECOMMENDATIONS

"See Me Through" by Tim Reimherr from *Immersed*

"I Trust You" by Justin Frederick from *Simple Devotion*

DAY 17

Coming Out of Hiding

LISA GOTTSHALL

Blessed are the poor in spirit,
for theirs is the kingdom of heaven.

MATTHEW 5:3 (ESV)

Has God ever dumbfounded your pride with His love? It had been a hard day. I'd been avoiding God all day, and I knew it. I wanted to fill my pain with food or something else that afforded immediate relief. That evening, I had an unusual stirring to take communion. Immediately, I thought, *No, I can't do that. It's not a good day for this.* And that's when it hit me: "On the night He was betrayed, the Lord Jesus took the bread" (1 Cor. 11:23). *God! You chose to offer all of yourself to those guys on the very night they would desert you— right there in their weakness and failure.*

I don't like feeling my need. But it's always there—a deep powerlessness that triggers my pride, to hide, pretend, and control. My pride is seen in the way I talk to my kids when they publicly embarrass me. It's revealed when I tell a close friend I'm fine when I'm not, or when

I stick with my safe prayer list instead of breaking down in tears and telling God how I really feel.

The central need of the human heart is to know we are loved and pursued for relationship just as we are. God created us for this loving connection, and He has brought us into it (John 15:9; 17:22; 1 John 3:1; Rom. 5–8). However, we can carry a lot of shame that has *convinced* us (even if our minds and mouths say otherwise) that we are *not* fully loved and accepted until we "get it right." We hide our imperfections and keep trying harder. But we won't experience the extravagance of His love until we come out of hiding.

We're all needy and poor in various ways. To be "poor in spirit" is to stop hiding from the truth of our need.

God is not just interested in us knowing the truth in our heads; He wants it in our inmost parts (Ps. 51:6). We say we are fine, because we think we *ought* to be, especially after Jesus' sacrifice for us and the gift of His Spirit inside of us. But if we are *not* fine, then we are lying to pretend so, and shame continues to keep us locked up inside.

Jesus would rather we open up and just say what we're thinking to Him than hide behind biblical phrases (Matt. 15:8–9). Until we let out what's really inside, we won't be convinced His love goes to the depths of who we are.

We are like Peter—we only want to relate to Jesus with a clean face. We don't want Him to go to our filthy feet. But Jesus' response is something like this: "If you don't let me meet you where you're filthiest, you don't have me" (John 13:1–8). Once we *do* receive Him there, our hearts are undone by His extravagant kindness to us even in our immaturity. There, we encounter the Man who is full of grace and truth, the perfect expression of the Father's heart. Right there in our poverty, the kingdom is ours (Matt. 5:3).

Only when Peter ran headlong into his weakness and met Jesus there, was he able to love Him genuinely and sincerely, rather than superficially (John 21:15–19). Likewise, when we are honest before Him, we realize His love meets us there. The heaviness of pretense lifts. Peace comes.

What if we made it our daily habit to come into agreement with the Father's love amidst all our mistakes? Coming to Jesus in our poverty leads to maturity. We are fully loved and accepted by Him amidst all our weakness and failure. To *believe* and *receive* this is the key that unlocks our hearts to come out of hiding and to grow up in Him.

How do we come to Jesus in our poverty? We stop pretending with Him. We accept the truth that we are all "in process" and that He enjoys us in the process.

He knows the difference between rebellion and sincerity. He knows my heart. He knows I'm aching over the childish places in me where I am stuck. Instead of just trying harder, could I trust more?

Holy Spirit, help me to be honest and real with you
so that I can know you and trust you more.

**What is one sentence that sums up what you think about
yourself when you feel weak? Can you believe that the
songs below express the Father's heart for you? If so,
how would this help you to live "poor in spirit"?**

SONG RECOMMENDATIONS

"Be Kind to Yourself" by Andrew Peterson
from *The Burning Edge of Dawn*

"Reckless Love" by Cory Asbury
from *Reckless Love*

DAY 18

Your Words Create

VERONIKA AND SEBASTIAN LOHMER

When we put bits into the mouths of horses to make them
obey us, we can turn the whole animal. Or take ships as
an example. Although they are so large and are driven
by strong winds, they are steered by a very small rudder
wherever the pilot wants to go. Likewise, the tongue
is a small part of the body, but it makes great boasts.
Consider what a great forest is set on fire by a small spark.

JAMES 3:3–5 (NIV)

It was four years ago on a Sunday when we excitedly
received the news that Veronika was pregnant with our
first child.

But only a few days later, Veronika was admitted to
the hospital because her body couldn't keep down any
kind of food or liquid nourishment. During the whole nine
months of pregnancy, she was terribly sick and weak. We
spent countless moments together on the couch while
she wept from the overwhelming physical pain. Through
that time, we struggled because our perspective became
skewed and hope had become so small.

It was exactly at that time and on that battlefield of

hopelessness, sadness, and desperation when we began to speak out how great God is, His purpose for us, and that this child would be a child of joy and delight for us.

The more we came into alignment with God's promises, the more we looked confidently ahead to the future. Our perspective grew into joy and confidence, although the external circumstances hadn't changed.

Looking at our everyday lives, families, and jobs, we all know such moments and times when difficulties and problems seem to become larger than life. It's exactly at those times that we must turn our focus on God and the promises He's given to us—harnessing the power of our words to claim and speak out His promises.

Everything in this world came into existence through the Father's spoken word. By means of the pronounced and audible word, life was created. God has created us according to His image. This means we are told to do what He has done: to create through our words. It is our vocation to reign with our words.

This is what we chose to do during Veronika's very challenging pregnancy. Everything went fine with our baby boy. All the sickness was over the moment he was born, and we gave him the name Immanuel, because God was with us. He is now three years old and has a brother who is one.

In difficult, hopeless, depressing, painful, dangerous, and bad situations we are given the chance to proclaim and express the truth even though we feel totally different. We declare who God is, how great Jesus is, how

He sees us—and then we boldly declare the fantastic and perfect plans and promises which He has given us.

When we have the strength to take this step of belief and faith, an atmosphere of faith, hope, and confidence will arise. Amid difficult circumstances, we look to Him, for whom no wall is too big to pull down. Just as a relatively small rudder can turn a giant ship, we can direct our hearts with our spoken words. Once the rudder is set and the word has been spoken, the circumstances will change and our feelings will adjust course to match the new heading.

Father, you are such a brilliant leader! All your paths are perfect as well as your scheduling. I can come and approach you the way I am. Thank you for miracles as I believe in the power of your name and when I hold onto your promises. Give me the power and strength to cling to your Word in every circumstance. Holy Spirit, dwell inside me and help me to look to you, my great helper.

Proclaim the truth of God over a difficult situation loudly and audibly and look and see what happens.

SONG RECOMMENDATIONS

"Cover Me" by Laura Hackett Park
from *Love Will Have Its Day*

"I Have Decided" by Don Potter from *Warfare*

DAY 19

Words of Life

BRANDON OAKS

"It is the Spirit who gives life; the flesh profits nothing. The words that I speak to you are spirit, and they are life." ... But Simon Peter answered Him, "Lord, to whom shall we go? You have the words of eternal life."

JOHN 6:63, 68

Words are powerful. Sometimes they bring you down; sometimes they lift you up. I remember as a kid being very upset about being very behind in school and not learning as fast as the other kids. My father sat down with me and spoke life into the thoughts in my head that were speaking death. Thoughts that I wasn't good enough or that I was stupid were replaced with *You are gifted*, and *You will overcome this*.

God does the same thing to us. He replaces lies with truth. When the accusing voice comes to steal, kill, and destroy, Jesus has the power to silence him. All wickedness starts from these small thoughts. God loves us so much that he will completely demolish the lies and words from the enemy.

Scripture shows us the power of God's words. He made all of creation by speaking words. He raised Lazarus from the dead by shouting, "Lazarus, come forth!" Miracles were performed because God spoke to a human and he or she obeyed. In Exodus 14, God told Moses to hold his hand over the sea. When he obeyed, the Red Sea began to part. In the Gospels, Jesus' spoken words brought life to many and continue to change millions of people even to this day. These God-spoken truths are what carry us and give us eternal life to the fullest. Jesus said, "I am the resurrection and the life. He who believes in Me, though he may die, he shall live. And whoever lives and believes in Me shall never die. Do you believe this?" (John 11:25–26).

Intentionality is the key. I will intentionally set up times with my worship team where we encourage one another. It's incredible to see how their hearts come alive as they give and receive encouragement. The days that I intentionally try and lift people up are the days where I myself am encouraged and those words will impact people's hearts more than anyone will ever know.

We ourselves have the power to speak life. The Bible says we have the same power that raised Christ from the dead living on the inside of us. He has given us the authority to speak His words and speak life each day. We have the power to overcome darkness and death with the power of the Holy Spirit. When we use this power, there is nothing—not death, demons, lies, or darkness—that can stand against us.

Lord, write your words on my heart so that I speak life and not death. Help me to use the power of your Word to break through every lie of the enemy. Fill my mouth with your words of eternal life to bring life to those around me.

In what areas do you want God to show you the truth? Who are a few people you want to hear the words of Christ?

SONG RECOMMENDATIONS

"Even When" by Brandon Oaks
from *Onething Live: All Cry Glory*

"All I Need" by Olivia Buckles
from *Fully Alive*

DAY 20

Keep Singing

JUSTIN RIZZO

> Therefore we do not lose heart. Though outwardly we
> are wasting away, yet inwardly we are being renewed
> day by day. For our light and momentary troubles are
> achieving for us an eternal glory that far outweighs
> them all. So we fix our eyes not on what is seen,
> but on what is unseen, since what is seen is temporary,
> but what is unseen is eternal.
>
> 2 CORINTHIANS 4:16–18 (NIV)

Who wants to hear sermons about suffering? I mean, really? I'd much rather hear a sermon about ten steps to joy, or talk about how to have a happy, pain-free life. Wouldn't you?

In 2005, the Lord began changing my perspective and removing the blinders over my eyes related to pain, suffering, and loss. It was a life-changing year. Because of that difficult season, I now call 2 Corinthians 4:16–18 one of the most beautiful passages in Scripture.

During those twelve months, I studied, sang, and prayed this passage repeatedly until I eventually found myself in the story that Paul so masterfully describes.

For Paul, his affliction was being persecuted for the gospel, beaten with rods, shipwrecked, and whipped. What kind of perspective did he have in order to call these *momentary* and *light* experiences? How is that possible?

What I was going through wasn't nearly as graphic as Paul's suffering, yet I was rebuking the enemy and doing anything I could to numb the pain. I was ready to throw in the towel.

I love the simplicity of this passage because it clearly gives us what we need to understand Paul's perspective. It's not a parable requiring hours in a commentary to understand. It's simple. Keep your eyes fixed on things you cannot see. What a command. You're telling me my solution to this affliction is to look at a God I can't see and an eternal reward that I believe in by faith?

This is so countercultural. In our McDonald's drive-thru, 24/7 convenience, Insta Story world, it really goes against the grain to tell people, *Fix your eyes on what you cannot see*. But truly, that is the way to true life.

God doesn't want us to be robots who shut down our hearts and emotions. On the contrary, He wants us to experience life to the fullest in this age. When we do, we're opening ourselves up to the pain of sorrow, loss, and regret. The fullness we seek must include being fully present—living and experiencing this age while setting our eyes on eternity.

I want to pass on a piece of advice that Mike Bickle

gave me during my difficult season in 2005—*Keep singing. Keep singing and never stop.*

In our weakest, darkest moments, the enemy tries to shut our mouths and tell us we deserve the difficulty, that it's our fault, that God is mad at us, and many other lies. The way to tear down the lies is with the Word of God. Singing God's Word over and over deposits it in our hearts and changes our perspective.

God, help me keep my heart always open to you. During painful seasons of loss or regret, I will keep singing and not lose heart. I want to live with my eyes fixed upon the eternal glory you have waiting for me.

What's one area of your life where you're experiencing pain today? Take out your Bible, turn to this passage or another Scripture that speaks to you, and spend two or three minutes singing the truth of God's Word over your life and situation.

SONG RECOMMENDATIONS

"Momentary Light Affliction" by Justin Rizzo
from *Found Faithful*

"Found Faithful" by Justin Rizzo
from *Found Faithful*

Section 3

The Journey
of Intimacy

DAY 21

Divine Identity

MATT GILMAN

When I consider Your heavens, the work of Your fingers,
The moon and the stars, which You have ordained,
What is man that You are mindful of him,
And the son of man that You visit him?
For You have made him a little lower than the angels,
And You have crowned him with glory and honor.
PSALM 8:3–5

I dreamed of being an astronaut when I was a kid. In
fifth grade there was a guest teacher who came in with
a portable planetarium, which took up nearly half the
basketball court in our gymnasium. I crawled inside with
my other classmates to wait in the pitch black for the
inflatable dome to be illuminated by a projection of all
the stars and planets that we could see with our limited
technology. I felt like I was floating in the outer expanse
of the universe.

Those childhood dreams of being a deep space
explorer seemed as if they became a reality in that

moment. I listened intently as the guest instructor showed us the formation of the constellations, told us the names of the stars, and spoke of the infinite amount of information that we could never possibly know about the universe because it was just so vast. Did you know that there are over 100 billion known galaxies that we have discovered? And did you also know that in each of those known galaxies there are anywhere from 100 billion to 400 billion stars?

Now imagine a young boy named David, living in the hills of Bethlehem, watching a herd of sheep in the middle of the night while gazing up at the beauty of hundreds of billions of stars with no ambient city light to dilute the raw majesty of the Lord's creation. What revelations did he receive about God as he spent those lonely nights on the hillside with nothing but his sheep and his harp? What songs did he sing as he peered into the galaxies?

It was in those moments that David would begin to ask God some real and honest questions. *When I consider your heavens, who am I that you are mindful of me? Why would you even think about me when you have such other beauty to look at?*

These are probably questions many of us have pondered. What is it about me that would cause the Creator of the universe to peer through hundreds of billions of galaxies just to get a glimpse of little, insignificant me? It doesn't make sense. After all I've done, haven't I disqualified myself from receiving any attention from the Almighty?

But David quickly, by divine revelation, answers his own questions. As God would speak to him, he would begin to realize his place of honor and dignity before the Lord. Did you know that you are the only creature in all of created order that bears the image of God? Did you know that you have been crowned with glory and honor by the Lord Himself? Did you know that you have been adopted into a royal family?

There is nothing that you could ever do to disqualify yourself from your position of honor and dignity. Take it from David because he surely knew. This was a man who committed murder, adultery, and then other sins that we can identify with on a more daily basis. But David was not defined by his struggles or his shortcomings. God said, *He is a man after my own heart.* In the same way, you are not defined by your struggles and shortcomings. By the blood of Jesus and by the power of His cross, you have been qualified to partake in a heavenly inheritance.

Remind yourself today of your identity in Him. You are royalty. You were not made for table scraps or crumbs that fall to the ground. You have been crowned by God with glory and honor. As one who bears His image, you have the highest place of dignity in His kingdom. You were the dream of His heart from eternity past. And right now, in this very moment, your Father is gazing over the balcony of Heaven, through all of the hundreds of billions of galaxies … to look right at you. And He's beaming with pride.

Father, remind me today of who you say I am. Show me how valuable I am to you and reveal the depths of your immeasurable love for me.

What does the Lord say about you right now in the specific circumstances of your own life? Take time today to write down these divine truths and revisit them as often as needed to remind yourself of your value and worth.

SONG RECOMMENDATIONS

"Awaken Love" by Matt Gilman
from *Awaken Love*

"More Than Ashes" by Tim Reimherr
from *Let the Weak Speak*

DAY 22

His Desire for Friendship

JON THURLOW

Thus the Lord used to speak to Moses face to face, just as a man speaks to his friend. When Moses returned to the camp, his servant Joshua, the son of Nun, a young man, would not depart from the tent.

EXODUS 33:11 (NASB)

When I was in my early teens, being a Christian meant two things: be a good kid, and spend five minutes a day reading your Bible. That's as far as it went. A set of values, a basic way to do life. And I was content with this. I wasn't dissatisfied with life and didn't feel a huge gap. This was Christianity, and that was that.

I think many sincere believers carry a similar approach. Being a Christian means doing what's right, avoiding what's wrong, and then praying or reading your Bible a bit here and there. That's as far as their faith goes.

But this all changed for me at the age of seventeen. I found myself in a teen Bible study, led by a nineteen-year-old guy who kept talking about God like they were friends. That was an *entirely* new idea to me. In the Bible study, we'd spend an hour in worship, which was way longer than what I'd been used to up to that point. But they weren't just singing songs. They were connecting with a person. People would be on their faces, standing, sitting, dancing, reading the Bible, or singing. Sometimes during worship, the leader would sit in a corner with his Bible. I later realized that he was listening for what the Lord might highlight to him to share that night. The whole thing was all so new to me.

Over the course of six months, my relationship with God changed. There wasn't some intense crisis moment—just this gradual realization that God was personal, and He wanted friendship with His people. Yes, He did want me to live according to the values of Scripture and to read my Bible. But it was out of a place of friendship, intimacy, and relationship with Him. God moved from occupying a compartment in my life, to being the center of my life—everything else revolved around that. In John 17, Jesus prayed to the Father that we "would be with Him" where He is, that we might see His glory. When I was seventeen, I began the journey of "being with Him."

I began to spend a lot more time with the Lord. When I wasn't with my family, when I wasn't doing schoolwork, when I wasn't practicing piano, I would try to get alone—just to be with God. I would journal and pray. I have vivid memories of being in high school, sitting on my bed at night where I would unpack my whole day with the Lord. I would talk to Him about everything. As a freshman in college, no matter how full my school day was, even if it was 11 p.m. and I was fried from homework and piano practice, I would still sit in the hallway outside my freshman dorm room and read and pray and listen, and just sit there in the Lord's presence. Not because I had heard lots of teaching on intimacy with Jesus—listening for the Lord, waiting upon Him, opening up my heart to Him—because at that point, I hadn't. The simple idea that God wanted friendship with me naturally brought those kinds of responses out of my heart.

Today I wonder how differently we, as God's people, would interact with Him if we knew He wanted friendship with us—if we knew Jesus wanted us with Him where He is. How much more time would we spend in His presence, in His Word, in stillness listening for His voice—if we knew that the Lord wanted close relationship with us?

Lord, speak to me today about your desire for friendship with me, and about your desire for me to be with you where you are.

What could you do today to become more aware of the Lord's desire for friendship with you?

SONG RECOMMENDATIONS

"Give Into Me" by Laura Hackett Park
from *Laura Hackett Park*

"I Want to Know You" by Jon Thurlow
from *Heat of Your Gaze*

DAY 23

The Good Father

JAYE THOMAS

"If you then, being evil, know how to give good gifts to your children, how much more will your Father who is in heaven give good things to those who ask Him!"

MATTHEW 7:11

Doctors had given my father twenty-four to forty-eight hours to live. But after eight days of my brother and I standing by his bed—each squeezing a hand that couldn't return the sentiment—our father died. It has been said that we most often relate to God the Father through the lens of our experience with our earthly fathers. Growing up in the Charismatic stream of the church, I heard people refer to God as "Abba" or "Daddy." It spoke of tenderness, kindness, approachability, acceptance, and immeasurable love. While my dad did his best and worked hard to provide us with a nice home, clothes, food, and cars, I didn't experience those attributes in my relationship with him.

Jesus came to earth for one purpose—to make known to us what the Father is like. The testimony of what I call the "New Testament 1s" confirms this—John 1:14, Romans 1:4, Galatians 1:1-4, Ephesians 1:17, Philippians 1:11, Colossians 1:3-11, and more. In Matthew 7 we find Jesus talking to his friends, the disciples, and helping them see with whom they are relating. I would have loved to have seen the look on their faces at the revelation that Jesus—their friend, teacher, healer, and source of infinite wisdom—is a son. This unique Son has a Father and is the representative of His Father's kingdom. Jesus is the manifestation of the good news that the Father is relational and desires to give to us all that He has of Himself. He desires to display His nature to us when we ask Him to.

There are countless ways in which the first person of the Trinity has revealed himself throughout history in the Bible. But more often than not, the Father is often seen as being angry and impatient. This understanding could be based on stories like Noah and the flood, Sodom and Gomorrah, and other Old Testament passages where we see Him display strength and power through His wrath. It is vital to understand the context in which He displayed His wrath. In every case, it was after He had displayed an abundance of kindness, mercy, patience, and even after declaring that He would change His plans if one righteous person could be found (see Genesis 18 and Jeremiah 5).

Perhaps fathers often get a bad rap because *the* Father has gotten one. There is so much more to who He is than meets the eye or experience. I recently heard a friend say, "It took becoming a father to really know how to be a son." I can attest to that. My dad wasn't a perfect man. He had many faults. But now that I have become a father, I have learned from my dad many priceless things. Perhaps the most important is that being a good father isn't *only* about providing things, but providing myself. "Things" come with the job and is standard operating equipment. But my children find themselves when I give myself to them.

This is the example of God our Father. He gives good gifts, but the greatest gift He gives is Himself—an understanding of and relationship with a gentle, kind, patient, and merciful Father. Upon this revelation, we find ourselves and the confidence to approach Him time and again. He is, in fact, a good, good Father.

Father, thank you for your steadfast love for me. Thank you for displaying your character through your Son, Jesus. Thank you that there is no disappointment in you. You delight to give good gifts because you are a good Father. Today, I lay aside my preconceived ideas about who you are. I will not accuse your character because my father was broken. I make a statement of faith regardless of what is happening in my life that you are good and your love endures! Help me to live like I believe this today and every day.

In what ways have you discovered God to be a good Father beyond what He can give you?

SONG RECOMMENDATIONS

"Family" by Jaye Thomas
from *Onething Live: All Cry Glory*

"You Give" by Clay Edwards
from *Night and Day*

DAY 24

Unquenchable Love

LAURA HACKETT PARK

Many waters cannot quench love,
neither can floods drown it.

SONG OF SOLOMON 8:7A (ESV)

And as we live in God, our love grows more perfect.
So we will not be afraid on the day of judgment,
but we can face him with confidence
because we live like Jesus here in this world.

Such love has no fear, because perfect love expels all
fear. If we are afraid, it is for fear of punishment, and this
shows that we have not fully experienced his perfect love.

1 JOHN 4:17-18 (NLT)

Is it inevitable? Do the floods have to come?

I hate pain. I hate feeling out of control. I hate
working towards something only to have it seem like it's
falling through. I hate when there is a death of any kind.
Let's be honest; don't we all? Verses like Matthew 7:25—
"and the floods came, and the winds blew and beat on
that house" (ESV)—feel terrifying at times. It's like living

in a floodplain and waiting for the next move of waters to pass over. I know this is the wrong part of the verse to focus on, but still, it says, "floods come," so how do I not live my life in fear about the next big wave?

I have spent a lot of life bracing myself for pain and worried about how I would be able to survive if this or that happened to me. Even during painful situations, I tend to seize up and panic while thinking, *I'm not going to make it.* Sometimes I wonder if the fear of pain itself is a flood the enemy causes.

It doesn't take much discernment to see this is not the way God intended us to live. Jesus finishes the passage in Matthew 7 by explaining that "if our house is built on the rock" we will not be shaken. He is so kind, and even when He addresses difficulties of life, He always gives us a reason to hope and not fear. 1 John 4:17 says, "Perfect love casts out fear" (ESV). So, if I am living afraid of the future, then that means I have not fully experienced God's perfect love.

I spent many days singing and meditating on this passage of how "love can cast out fear" and how "many waters cannot quench love," but I still felt like I was getting stuck. It wasn't until the Holy Spirit began to speak to me about how love matures over time that I began to receive a breakthrough in the arena of fear. A continual receiving of the fire of God's love is the impetus that "turns up the heat" and brings those deep fears and negative thoughts to the surface.

Some of the keys for me in overcoming fear and

letting God's love be my life's foundation have been: Repent. Resist. Replace. These are three handy "Rs" the Lord has used to mature love in me. First, repentance has been so key for me! Yes, fear is a manifestation of a wrong belief about God, so I first must repent for any and all agreement with a lie about God or myself. Second, I resist or rebuke the spirit that is behind fear. The Bible says there is a "spirit of fear," and a lot of times when something feels heightened emotionally it is a demonic spirit seeking to oppress us. The Bible simply tells us in James 4:7 to "resist the devil and he will flee." Third, I search God's Word and ask the Holy Spirit to replace the lie I was believing with His truth.

Receiving God's truth despite our fears is like gathering more building material for our house upon the Rock. It's like pouring gasoline on the fire of God's love in us. In one of my most-read passages, John 16:33, Jesus says, "Here on earth you will have many trials and sorrows. But take heart, because I have overcome the world" (NLT). Jesus is so kind to warn us of these things before they happen so we can have peace and remain in Him no matter what. Even as fears come to the surface in different seasons of our lives, we can see them as opportunities for our love to grow and mature.

Just as Jesus walked on the earth, we can have confidence that God's love in us cannot even be broken by death. For love is stronger than death and will last for all eternity.

Lord, come and baptize me with the fire of your love today. Thank you for fighting for my love to be mature and perfected. Help me experience your love in a deeper way.

Take a few moments to journal and apply the three "Rs" (repent, resist, replace) to any recent fear you have had in your life. Make sure to take time to write out the truth that the Holy Spirit reveals.

SONG RECOMMENDATIONS

"When I Am Afraid" by Laura Hackett Park
from *Laura Hackett*

"You Won't Relent" into "All-Consuming Fire"
by Misty Edwards
from *Relentless*

DAY 25

The God of Redemption

JON THURLOW

Who is a God like You, who pardons iniquity.
MICAH 7:18A (NASB)

It was one of the lowest points in my life. A strong season of pursuing the Lord was followed by three years of compromise. I was in my early twenties, backslidden, and I knew it. I didn't want to be where I was—I wanted to reconnect with the Lord, but I felt stuck. I didn't know how to break free of a lifestyle filled with the patterns and cycles of sin—an existence marked by an absence of a life in the secret place with the Lord. The feeble attempts I made had failed and I felt hopeless.

I moved to Kansas City and did an internship called Fire in the Night. With fifty other young adults, I slept morning and afternoon, took Bible classes at night, and spent from midnight to 6 a.m. in a prayer room every day. Kind of a crazy concept to many, but I chose it because I knew I needed something crazy to help push me back to God.

Honestly, it was a hard three months. Because my heart was dull and I was in such rough shape spiritually, I was constantly bucking up against the structure of the internship. Here I was, trying to renew my relationship with the Lord, and yet I was fighting the opportunities the internship afforded at every turn. Many moments that could have been spent in prayer and in the Word were spent watching movies and skipping prayer meetings.

And then the Lord broke in. I once heard a wise man say that if the Lord really wants to get our attention, He will shout (so to speak). And in this case, He shouted. I won't go into detail due to the personal nature of the experience, but the Lord got my attention. Through a series of divine setups, God opened a very clear door for me to stay long-term in Kansas City at the house of prayer. Things I never would have guessed could happen, did happen and I knew it was the Lord.

I didn't immediately walk through this open door. Probably about a month after my internship had ended, I was back at my parents' house in Colorado and in tears. I remember saying to God, *Why are you being nice to me? I've been a jerk the last several years, and have not been pursuing you. And now you're opening up a major door for me? Showing me favor? Why?!*

God didn't answer me in that moment, but He didn't have to. At the end of the day, I just knew the opportunity was from Him. I knew it was His favor and I knew I was going to go back to Kansas City to join the staff at the house of prayer.

In the fall of 2004, I joined the full-time staff at the house of prayer in Kansas City. It would be another year before my life in God really turned around, but this was a small step towards renewal—and God was showing me much grace and favor.

That season has become a precious testimony to me. God showed himself to me in a powerful way as the one who "pardons iniquity" (Mic. 7:18). At the end of the book of Micah, the prophet speaks of a day when Israel will inhabit their land and be prosperous again (Mic. 7:14–15). God's favor will rest upon them in such a way that the nations of the earth will be shocked. God's blessings will not only stand in contrast to the hard conditions of other nations (v. 13), but because Israel did not deserve this kind of favor (vv. 9, 18). The beauty of it all is that God is showing everyone that He is the God of redemption. He's convincing Israel of this, and He's convincing the earth of this!

When we take a tiny step toward the Lord, He runs a mile toward us. This is our God. When we are at our lowest, when it looks like there is no way forward, when we feel like we've let Him and everyone else down, He breaks in with abundant grace and favor to show us that He's the God of redemption.

Father, fill me with hope today. Show me that you are the God who redeems my hardest season and that you are the God of the breakthrough.

Think back on your own journey in the Lord. Remember back to the times when He broke in, however big or small the breakthrough seemed in the moment. Go back and remember, and let it fill you with hope for your current challenges and for the future. He broke through before, and He will break through again.

SONG RECOMMENDATIONS

"The Love Inside" by Laura Hackett Park
from *Love Will Have its Day*

"Every Movement" by Jon Thurlow
from *Walking Through the Night*

DAY 26

Make My Love
Your Home

ANNA BLANC

"As the Father loved Me, I also have loved you;
abide in My love."

JOHN 15:9

I can fake it like the best of them. There are days filled
with meetings, coffee with friends, work, and even
hours of singing with a worship team. Without even
realizing it, I can run on the fumes of optimism, and
hold up a facade of having it all together and fooling
everyone around me—even myself.

But the one place my fakery cannot stand is in
my home. Like Cinderella at midnight, the true me is
suddenly exposed and no one is fooled—certainly not
my husband or children. I'm the gut-level, authentic,
messy me. I remember the day clearly when I was
preparing to lead worship at IHOPKC. In my mind, I
see my open songbook, a candle burning, and my
heart preparing to lead a room full of people into His

presence. In reality? I had russet potatoes literally flying back and forth over my head as my boys waged war on either side of me, screaming, crying, while I threatened discipline at the top of my lungs. There is no hiding it; that is the real me.

In the book of John, Jesus is instructing His disciples in arguably the most important discourse recorded. He is a man on death row, knowing the grave is right around the corner, and He is sharing His legacy. His plea to the friends He had spent every day with for three years of His ministry is this: "Come home to my love. Let my love be home base, the place you run to. The place you let your hair down in all your true, raw, unkempt being."

So often our impulse is to clean ourselves up for God. He is Holy! I've seen just a glimpse of the impurity in my own heart. Even after years of being a Christian, I feel the struggles of comparison, the haughtiness of pride, the quickness of my temper. If I can just hold those things in, keep the flares of sin at bay while I am spending time with the Lord, then all the better, right? Instead, Jesus' plea flies in the face of this thinking. He has those blazing eyes of fire that look right into the core of me. He is not fooled by my polished exterior, my iron-tight defenses. He sees not as man sees, and He is looking at my heart. And right in the middle of that mess He is saying *Make my love your home. Let me in here, right in the middle of the mess.*

Throughout Scripture, Jesus reaches out to us in authenticity and simplicity, and He does it most clearly at the communion table. The night before His death, with fervent desire, He breaks the bread and lifts His cup of wine, asking His disciples to remember Him through these elements. We call them "sacraments" sometimes, but if we strip away the fancy language, it's really just food and drink. Not even special food. Just bread that was already on the table and would be on the table for most meals in those days. His death ... *His* death remembered by such a routine, simple action— one that even the poor, the uneducated do three times a day. And in this we see Him reaching for us. Past the pretenses. Through the facade. Into the mundane, the routine, the messy. He is sitting at the table with me in my home in the middle of lunchtime. He is picking up my peanut butter and jelly sandwich and saying, "Meet me here. This is where I want to meet with you. This is my divinely designated place of communion, where every breath is holy and every moment an opportunity for real, authentic relationship."

Jesus is saying to you, *Make my love your home.*

Lord Jesus, make your home with me. In the daily moments, both large and small, may I find my home in you. Thank you for your call that brings me into such sweet, intimate communion with you—removing the facade and finding my home in your love.

What part of your regular routine do you want to make Jesus a part of today?

SONG RECOMMENDATIONS

"Jesus My Brother" by Chris Tofilon
from *Fully Alive*

"Weak and Broken Vows" single by Anna Blanc

Sometimes We Forget That He Likes Us

JON THURLOW

> While he was still a long way off,
> his father saw him and felt compassion for him,
> and ran and embraced him and kissed him.
>
> LUKE 15:20B (NASB)

When my weaknesses and issues come to the surface, several things happen. I get surprised, because I didn't initially see the issue, and now I do. I get upset, because I wish the issue wasn't there. I get embarrassed, because I should know better. I make the issue bigger than it is. And then I get discouraged because I don't know what to do about it or how I'm going to overcome it. When I finally do begin to interact with the Lord about the issue, I approach Him with my walls up, assuming He's frustrated and upset with me. Suddenly, I hear His voice break into my internal swirl: *Jon, I still like you.*

In Luke 15, the prodigal son has a moment when the lights come on, and he realizes his sin. The text says, "he came to his senses" (v. 17). Then he makes the decision to leave his lifestyle of sin and return to his father. This is significant. We never want to minimize or overlook the necessity of acknowledging our sin, turning from it, and returning to the Lord. But if you're like me, you can get confused by the regret over your sin and lose perspective of how the Lord sees you and what He thinks about you.

I love Luke 15:20, where it describes the father's response to his son. It says, "While he was still a long way off, his father saw him and felt compassion for him, and ran and embraced him and kissed him" (NASB). Whoa! The father's perspective is a whole lot different than the son's. The son was hoping maybe his dad would let him work as a servant on the estate—which assumes that his dad was really angry at him over the whole thing, was going to make him pay, and would never treat him like a son again. Nothing could be further from the truth.

Jesus' story says the father saw him from a distance, which indicates that the father was watching, waiting, longing for his son. Then when the father does see his son, he *runs* to hug him, and immediately calls for a celebration to rejoice over him and reinstate him as a son.

Do we view the Lord this way when we blow it? Is this how we think He'll respond to us? Or have we forgotten that He *really* likes us? To be sure, it doesn't say anywhere in the text that the father overlooks or minimizes his son's sin or makes light of his son's repentance. And we know from other passages in

Scripture that these things are crucial. What's important to see here is that in the context of his son's utter weakness and brokenness, the father is *overcome with joy* by his return—because he loves *and likes* his son!

Some of us have heard this truth many times. But whether we're hearing it for the first time or the hundredth time, there is something in us that truly struggles to believe this when we're in the pit of our weakness. We're overwhelmed by our sin, and we need to hear the Father say this to us again. The Father knows this. He knows that we'll never graduate from needing to hear that He loves us as sons and daughters in His house. And so He tells us—over, and over, and over again.

Father, give me grace to hear your voice of love when I'm at my lowest. Remind me again what you see when you look at me, and how you feel about me.

What are some barriers that might hinder your ability to hear the Father's voice of compassion when you are at your lowest point? What are some things you can do to bypass or remove those barriers?

SONG RECOMMENDATIONS

"Confidence in Love" by Jon Thurlow
from *Heat of Your Gaze*

"Mighty Hand" by Jon Thurlow
from *Heat of Your Gaze*

DAY 28

Holy Spirit Inside You

JUSTIN RIZZO

"But the Advocate, the Holy Spirit, whom the Father
will send in my name, will teach you all things and will
remind you of everything I have said to you."

JOHN 14:26 (NIV)

Upstairs in my home I have a writing room. It's
where I go to work on all sorts of writing projects,
including the devotional you're reading right now.
About five minutes after sitting down to write this,
my thoughts were interrupted by the neighborhood
weather siren announcing a tornado warning in our area.
After grabbing my wife and kids and spending forty-five
minutes in our basement, the storm has passed, the kids
are peaceful, and I'm back in my writing room.

As my family took cover in the basement, my
thoughts kept returning to John 14:26. For years, I
thought of Jesus as my friend when I was at church on
Sunday, during a worship service, or a prayer meeting.
But in reality, it's in the everyday moments that He
wants to be my friend. He's looking for relationship

when I'm going about business as usual, when a weather scare causes my family to seek shelter, and all the moments in between. It's in these memorable and not-so-memorable moments that the Lord wants to talk with me.

More specifically, the Holy Spirit.

It's easy to hear about "a relationship with God" and just gloss over that phrase because it feels so ambiguous. I want to take a moment to tell you what it has come to mean to me.

Paul says in Ephesians 1:13 that after hearing the gospel and believing, we receive the Holy Spirit. If you've been in church, you've probably heard this referred to as "being marked in Christ" or "sealed by the Holy Spirit".

Like many believers, I grew up familiar with the concept of "receiving the Spirit," but what does that really mean?

When you accept the gospel, the third person of the Trinity comes and makes His home inside you. Your once-dead spirit is awakened and made alive in Christ and you become "born again" (John 3:3–6). Scripture says the uncreated God dwelling within you is the core reality of this new birth (1 Cor. 6:17, 1 John 3:8–9). We are reborn into a whole new dimension of connectedness with the Holy Spirit (John 3:4).

God didn't die on a cross to save you just so you could get your foot in the door of heaven. He wants you to fully enter in. When a friend invites you into his house, you don't just stay in the doorway. You come in, look around, and experience what's inside. Your salvation was God's invitation to come in and explore all He has for you.

God's desire is that you would live life in constant communication with the indwelling Spirit—have intimate access to God because the Spirit inside us is the glory of every believer. I call communing or talking to the Spirit within us "fellowshipping with the Spirit" (2 Cor. 13:14). This isn't complicated. It's actually so simple that we overlook or forget it. But talking to God within us is the core foundation that sustains all believers.

This reality—an abiding, intimate, ongoing conversation with the Holy Spirit—is the key to taking ourselves, our families, and our worship teams to the next level.

Holy Spirit, thank you for living inside me and always wanting to talk with me. Help me slow down and talk to the Friend who is closer than a brother and make this my practice all of my days.

Take five minutes right now to talk to the Holy Spirit inside you. What is He saying to you right now? Thank Him for who He is and what He does. Ask Him for wisdom and strength. Talk to Him about whatever is on your mind right now and be still to listen for His response.

SONG RECOMMENDATIONS:

"About You" by Justin Rizzo
from *Savior's Love*

"Rest in My Savior's Love" by Justin Rizzo
from *Savior's Love*

DAY 29

The Muscle of Discernment

LAURA HACKETT PARK

And this I pray, that your love may abound still more
and more in knowledge and all discernment.

PHILIPPIANS 1:9

For everyone who partakes only of milk is unskilled in
the word of righteousness, for he is a babe. But solid
food belongs to those who are of full age, that is, those
who by reason of use have their senses exercised to
discern both good and evil.

HEBREWS 5:13–14

I go in and out of seasons of working out my body.
When I was younger, I could run around, play soccer,
eat whatever I wanted, and not really have to worry
about anything. The older I get, the wear and tear of
living weigh on me. If I spend even a few weeks in a
sedentary lifestyle now, suddenly new aches and pains
I didn't even know existed come to the surface. I find I
do best when at least a couple of times a week I spend

focused time working out muscle groups that regularly need attention and strengthening.

In the same way, the more mature I grow in the Lord, the more aware I am of spiritual forces that weigh heavy and weaken my spiritual frame. The apostle Paul tells a young Timothy to be a good soldier because we are living in a battle (2 Tim. 2:3). The apostle Peter describes our enemy, Satan, as a roaring lion seeking whom he may devour (1 Peter 5:8). Phew! Verses like these remind me that I really can't coast through life and expect to stay strong in the Spirit. There is a proactive stance the Bible calls us to take in order to keep our strength or gain even more. So how do we stay active in the Spirit?

Hebrews 5:12–14 describes our need for spiritual discernment using the example of a baby. Babies need someone to feed them milk in order to survive, but as they get older, they no longer wait passively for someone to feed them. We too must actively use the resources that are given to us to grow stronger.

We all consume to survive, but the question is, *What are we consuming*? Does it strengthen, drain, incite anxiety, or bring peace? When I am walking in true discernment, I am aware of my God-given needs and I take responsibility for what I choose to fill myself with. I believe this is where true discernment and growth begins in the Spirit. Just like a healthy person eats the right food and exercises to stay strong, so a believer receives truth and exercises discernment to stay healthy in our fallen world. Our spiritual being must be fed by actively partaking of the resources God has provided—the Bible and prayer.

For me personally, it is in a moment of crisis or weakness that reveals my need for discernment. I ask simple questions like *Lord, is there an open door of sin right now that is giving the enemy a foothold?* or *Have I fed myself on something harmful?* or *What is your perspective right now, Lord?* I also search the Scriptures and biblical stories for the revelation of truth that could apply to what is going on in my life.

True discernment is knowing what God is thinking. God's perspective about what is happening is what we are after! But many of us forget to ask Him or give Him any time to respond.

In my experience, the Lord faithfully shows me something I need to repent of or someone I need to forgive in order to see clearer and make healthier decisions for my life. Sin and unforgiveness can cloud my vision and make it harder to resist temptation thrown at me by the world and people around me. Daily repentance is a necessary activity for my spiritual walk. Once I am in a place of being right with God, I find that His ways and thoughts are amplified and made clear to me.

1 John 4:1 tells us to actively "test the spirits," and in chapter 5 we are encouraged to have confidence that God hears our questions and will answer. We really can have an anointing from the Holy One to discern both good and evil in every circumstance and situation. Let us start exercising this gift as the church, for confusion is never our portion!

Thank you, my Lord, that confusion is not my portion but rather power, love, and clarity of mind. Tell me your thoughts and show me your perspective on my life right now in this moment.

Take a moment to ask the Lord a question about something you have felt confused by in life. Then write down anything you hear, see, or any Scripture you start to think of. (Sometimes I find the answer comes later in the day unexpectedly after a time of waiting.)

SONG RECOMMENDATIONS

"Tree" by Justin Rizzo
from *Found Faithful*

"Judgments are Better Than Gold" by Justin Rizzo
from *Found Faithful*

DAY 30

Your Home in the Throne Room

JON THURLOW

> Immediately I was in the Spirit;
> and behold, a throne was standing in heaven.
>
> REVELATION 4:2A (NASB)

Years ago, I heard IHOPKC director, Mike Bickle, share that when he would pray, he would often picture God's throne room as described in Revelation 4. That stood out to me, and I decided I would try it myself. Each day I began setting aside time in my devotions to pray in the Spirit around Revelation 4 and visualize that throne room scene. Little did I know that it was going to dramatically change my life in God.

Each morning, I would go phrase by phrase through Revelation 4, speaking it out loud to the Lord and putting it in the form of thanks. When the text would read, "a throne was standing in heaven," I would repeat it by saying, "God, thank you that there is a throne standing in heaven." Then I would pray in the Spirit for a bit and move on to the next phrase. The whole time I was picturing that throne room and then picturing myself before the Lord as I prayed.

I don't fully understand it, but as I began to pray through Revelation 4 consistently, there was something about telling the Lord "thank you" for each phrase I was saying that removed any question about its truth, and instead put an exclamation point on it as a fact. In other words, it solidified the reality of that throne room and of the One who inhabits that holy place. I knew that I knew there was a throne and One seated on the throne. I also noticed how it brought my heart into a place of gratitude. It was like my spirit came alive on the inside through agreeing with the truth of the phrase—and was shouting, *Yes! Amen!*

At the same time this was all happening, the challenges of life that were weighing so heavily on my mind went from being huge problems to much smaller issues in light of the truth. It's like the Holy Spirit would whisper to me, *There's a throne standing in heaven, and God is on the throne. It's going to be okay.*

Then I would come to verse 3, where it says God has the appearance of a jasper stone. This phrase has probably been the one that has most consistently impacted my heart over the years. A jasper stone is clear—transparent. There's nothing in it that clouds or colors its appearance. It points to the Father's purity and perfection. He has no sin, no flaws, and is completely holy. The longer I live, the more aware I am of my own weakness and frailty and the weakness and frailty of others. My heart, and every other human heart, is looking for interaction—for connection with someone who is completely stable, clean, pure, perfect, and completely holy. We only find this in the Father.

As I began to connect with the Father—the one who is perfect, clean, and righteous—something unlocked in my heart, something that I wasn't even aware was locked up. My guard came down and my heart opened up, because I knew it would be safe with Him. Nothing in the world compares with our hearts opening and connecting with God the Father in this way. It's what we were made for.

I discovered that Revelation 4 has become like a home for me. It is where I connect with the Lord, where my heart is realigned with truth, and where divine perspective on life takes place. It's been over a decade since I began to pray through the throne room scene, and I can't imagine what my life would have looked like otherwise.

God, continually draw me into your throne room, into your presence. Please give me grace to keep coming back, over and over again.

How have you reached to connect with God through the Revelation 4 throne room? What could you do today to meet with Him in this way?

SONG RECOMMENDATIONS

"Storm All Around You" by Jon Thurlow
from *Onething Live: Magnificent Obsession*

"As I Am Holy" by Jon Thurlow
from *Heat of Your Gaze*

Section 4

The Fullness
of Life

DAY 31

The Wonder of a Childlike Heart

LAURA HACKETT PARK

"Truly, I say to you, whoever does not receive the kingdom of God like a child shall not enter it."

MARK 10:15 (ESV)

Then I looked, and behold, a whirlwind was coming out of the north, a great cloud with raging fire engulfing itself; and brightness was all around it and radiating out of its midst like the color of amber, out of the midst of the fire. Also from within it came the likeness of four living creatures ... And above the firmament over their heads was the likeness of a throne, in appearance like a sapphire stone; on the likeness of the throne was a likeness with the appearance of a man high above it.

EZEKIEL 1:4–5, 26

It's amazing to me how often we like to pretend we understand someone or something. We can't handle questions or mystery when we become adults. The need to feel in control and on top of information is innate to the human mind, but with the mass availability of information on the internet, the art of searching and ruminating on questions seems to be fading. We read just one blog or book and suddenly we are talking with our friends like we are the expert! This causes us to be all too critical of someone else's perspective before we truly understand the information. I have found myself jumping so quickly to conclusions on subjects and people's statements that the awareness of my need to learn has become impaired. Thank you, God, for the whisper of the Holy Spirit in our lives to pull us off the wrong way of living. *You must become like a child*, is what I began to hear recently.

I love how simple and real Jesus is when explaining to us how to live in the kingdom of God. In Mark 10:15, the adults were fighting about who was the greatest and looking for ways to feel justified in the midst of sin. They didn't want the distraction of kids in their important meetings and Jesus rebuked them saying, "Not only do I want to spend time with these children, but if you adults don't become like them, you can never enter into God's kingdom." Wow! What does this mean?

Like all revelation from God, there are layers that we could spend lifetimes uncovering. I understood this much more when I became a mom. For example, spending a day with a small child demonstrates that children observe the world with wonder and simplicity. Nothing misses a child's eye. They often don't know how to interpret what they are seeing and hearing, but they are observing what most adults pass right by. "The moon, Mommy!" "An airplane!" "Mommy, are you sad?"

Second, they question ... incessantly. It's hilarious to me how many times I can answer the same question over and over in a day, but my child's curiosity about the world around us makes me stop and think because a lot of times I don't know the answer.

Lastly, children have a sense of trust even in the mystery. The questioning and lack of understanding in life doesn't bring defeat, depression, or the need to control, but instead brings a sense of wonder and imagination that propels them into deeper learning and relationship. Lord, help me live like that!

I am guessing that Ezekiel 1 has to be one of the most skipped-over passages in the Bible. What is happening? There are crazy-looking creatures, wheels inside other wheels, a burning whirlwind storm with an amber and sapphire center, raging thunderous noises, and more. This passage is mysterious and past my understanding. There is a fear of the unknown that can cause me to run from or discount passages like this.

When God came and visited the prophets of old, many of them ended up on the ground "like a dead man," unable to move or speak because they were so afraid. They often needed the Spirit to lift them up or an angel to strengthen them just so they could continue to talk with God in the moment. It can be a very scary feeling when you do not understand what is happening around you. Here is where the perspective of a child can be so immensely helpful.

The fearful and mysterious revelations of God don't have to scare us into hiding from Him. If we live like we are children of God, the fearful, awe-inspiring wonder can lead us to deeper worship. The simplicity of asking our Father questions without inhibition will draw us into the sweetest moments of communion with Him. Even whirlwind-scary seasons can be an invitation into wonder and worship, as we, like children, know that He delights in us, in spite of our repeated questions.

We can trust the mysterious adventure God is bringing into our lives. We can trust the invitation to learn biblical passages that are harder to readily understand. Sometimes, like the prophets, we need the strengthening of the Spirit to continue and remain in a moment with God. But one thing is for certain: we will never be bored if we live in the wonder of a childlike heart!

Lord, help me live with the wonder of a child and not fear the questioning or mysterious nature of who you are.

Ask the Lord to show you a time when the fear of the unknown stole the wonder of worship from you. Take a moment to remember that time and write down what you see.

SONG RECOMMENDATIONS

"Ezekiel 1" by Luke Wood
from *The Sound of War*

"How Awesome Are Your Works" by Laura Hackett Park
from *Fully Alive*

DAY 32

Worship Is Warfare

ROBBY ATWOOD

God's high and holy praises fill their mouths, for their shouted praises are their weapons of war! These warring weapons will bring vengeance on every opposing force and every resistant power—to bind kings with chains and rulers with iron shackles. Praise-filled warriors will enforce the judgment-doom decreed against their enemies. This is the glorious honor he gives to all his godly lovers. Hallelujah! Praise the Lord!

PSALM 149:6–9 (TPT)

Imagine with me that the President has just gone live on TV across the country to address the nation. Enemies are pressing in, hurling threats at our land, and the threat calls for immediate action. The nation eagerly waits to hear what the Commander in Chief is going to say. How will he respond to the impending danger? What charge will he give the troops? What comfort will he offer to his people?

After general remarks, he proceeds to call the nation to a time of seeking the Lord. Then he declares that all troops who happen to play an instrument, dance, or sing will be the foot soldiers to take their place at the front of the battle. He goes on to say that instead of pulling a weapon, they're going to play an instrument. Instead of lifting a hand in defense, they're going to lift their voices in praise. This is his plan: combat the enemy by worshiping the Lord.

Sounds a little crazy, huh? Well, this has happened before, and it turned out in triumphant victory!

Second Chronicles 20 tells us of a king who called a nation to the combat of worship. The "great multitude" of the Moabites, Ammonites, and Meunites joined together to make war against King Jehoshaphat. It was three against one. Verse 3 tells us that Jehoshaphat was afraid and turned his attention to seek the Lord. He then proclaimed a fast throughout all Judah. Instead of turning to his own military strength, this young king turned to God's strength.

In response to the Lord's voice, the young king hosted a corporate worship service—right in the midst of the enemy threat. Out of this gathering, "he appointed those who sang to the Lord and those who praised Him in holy attire" (20:21 NASB). The worshipers "went out before the army and said, 'Give thanks to the Lord, for His lovingkindness is everlasting.'"

Instead of swinging, they went singing. Instead of the usual violent approach, they lifted their voices in worship. Against the fervent attack of their enemies, they sang of God's everlasting lovingkindness. The Lord didn't instruct them to yell at devils or cast out demons, but to simply worship Him.

In response, the Lord set up an ambush against the opposing army. The furious praise of God's people routed the enemy—they actually began to turn on themselves. Their defeat had nothing to do with the violence of Jehoshaphat's army, but everything to do with Judah's willingness to worship the Lord. Their upward focus released horizontal conquest.

Their worship became a weapon in God's hand. The praise coming from their hearts became a dagger in the hearts of the enemy. It's quite obvious that the Lord could have defeated the enemies of Judah all by Himself, yet He chose to do so through the worship of His people. Their high praises became a channel for the Lord to release His mighty hand.

I believe this principle is still true today. He wants to use our worship as a weapon. Worship is warfare.

In Acts 16, Paul and Silas found themselves in prison but decided to praise the Lord anyway. It was at the midnight hour (the darkest time) that they began to lift their voices. And as they did, the Lord lifted His hand and broke open the doors. No longer were they captive behind bars, but they were free ... free by their song.

Friend, there is freedom in your song. I believe if you begin to view your obstacles as an opportunity to worship, things will happen. The enemy will begin to turn on himself when we turn to the Lord. Introduce your midnight hour to your worship and watch things happen. Watch the Lord take your humble song and begin to form a huge victory on your behalf. Allow your worship to become a weapon in God's hand.

Father, you are with me in every season of life—in the successes as well as the struggles. Through it all, I will choose to worship you, my strongest weapon.

When have you seen the Lord break through as you worshiped? Journal those times where He remained faithful as you worshiped.

SONG RECOMMENDATIONS

"The Battle is Raging/I Put on Christ"
by Laura Hackett Park
from *Onething Live: Where I Belong*

"Surrounded (Fight My Battles)" by Elissa Smith
from *Surrounded*

DAY 33

Fuel to Burn

JOSHUA ALDY

And they said to one another, "Did not our hearts burn within us while He talked with us on the way and while He opened to us the Scriptures?"

LUKE 24:32 (KJ21)

Have you ever tried to start a fire without a match? A while back, I was on a camping trip with three of my bros. We were so pumped to be in the great outdoors with only the bare necessities. Being men, we decided that on this trip we would start a fire using nothing but wood. No matches allowed. No lighter fluid. No paper ... you get the picture. It was man versus nature and we were determined to win. I won't say how long it took me, but with a little sweat and blood, and some good ol' wood, I started that fire!

Fire is a curious thing. Have you ever just sat and stared into one for a while? It's so alive! The fire dances and moves like nothing else. Yet, it's so delicate. If you don't constantly attend to it, the fire dies. It takes oxygen and wood to keep the fire burning bright.

Have you ever thought about what it takes for your heart to burn for Jesus? As a father of three, this verse in Luke 24 weighs heavily upon my heart. If I don't understand and obtain a heart that burns for the Lord, then my children will likely grow up to have hearts that are dead and dull too.

I believe a burning heart is deeply connected with hunger and the desire for more. The two men who traveled with Jesus and heard His words didn't want to part ways. Their seven-mile trek turned into an entire day's journey as this Man and His words gripped them. Even when the day was spent, they pleaded with Him to stay the night. It was this hungry passion they later recognized as the fire within their hearts!

But there's more to a burning heart than just hunger. That hunger must be fed. Like a vibrant fire, a burning heart can't survive unattended. From these verses in Luke 24, we see there were two things that made their hearts burn: their conversation with Jesus and the discussion of the Scriptures.

Simply put, it's prayer and the Word. Prayer isn't just one-way communication for specific needs. Although it includes making requests, prayer is the dialogue and conversation that we have with God. Us speaking to Him, and Him speaking back to us. That's true prayer. We can create conversation with God about His Word. It can be as simple as asking deeper questions about what you read or talking to Him about how these Scriptures can apply to your life. God loves to talk to you about His Word!

These two elements are the oxygen and fuel that feed the fire of the heart.

Before I started dialoguing with God about the Scriptures, reading my Bible sometimes felt like a boring chore. I didn't often connect or feel like I understood much afterwards. But when I began combining God's Word with prayer, it was like striking a match to the dead leaves in my heart! The Bible began to come alive to me and my heart started to burn for those times when God opened up the Scriptures for me, just like He did for the two men on the road to Emmaus.

Practically speaking, if you want a heart that's alive and burning for God, it comes down to having consistent time with Him—getting in the Word and talking about it with Him. Attending church once a week won't keep your heart alive, no more than a fire would be kept alive by dumping a few logs on it once a week.

The Word and prayer must work together. If all you do is read the Word but never dialogue with God about His Word, then your heart will burn mostly of religious zeal, like the Pharisees in Jesus' day (John 5:39–40). Likewise, if all you do is pray but never heed the truth in God's Word, you won't be able to stand against the lies of the culture and will be easily swept away (Matt. 7:24–27).

It's the combination of prayer and the Word of God that keeps our hearts alive and burning. I encourage you to daily spend time talking to God about what you read in His Word. It's that time in the secret place that will turn your heart into a bonfire for Jesus.

God, I want to burn for you. Let my whole being be
consumed with hunger and desire for more.
No worldly pleasure can compare with you. Help me
to daily read your Word and talk with you about it.
I ask for a heart that's alive in you, so let me burn.

**What does passionate hunger look like in your life?
When are specific times in your day that you could
dialogue with God?**

SONG RECOMMENDATIONS

"Heart after You" by Luke Wood
from *EP*

"What Only You Can Do" by Misty Edwards
from *Always on His Mind*

DAY 34

The Adventure
of Searching

JOHAN HEINRICHS

Making your ear attentive to wisdom
and inclining your heart to understanding; …
if you seek it like silver
and search for it as for hidden treasures,
then you will understand the fear of the Lord
and find the knowledge of God.

PROVERBS 2:2,4–5 (ESV)

When I was ten years old, my parents gave me the one thing I was asking for that year: a metal detector so I could go out searching for lost, buried treasure. Later in my teens, I would go for hikes in the woods and veer off the trail and say to myself, "I might have been the first person in history to step on this exact spot."

The movie *Raiders of the Lost Ark* captivated my imagination. The moment I saw Indiana Jones lift the glistening gold ark of the covenant out of its stone cradle, I felt a mysterious excitement and curiosity rise inside of me. I wanted to be on a quest to find something that was lost, something priceless. I wanted to uncover ancient mysteries and have an adventurous life full of fresh and new discoveries.

We may not all enjoy adventure stories and the quest for ancient civilizations, but in the heart of every person there is a desire for discovery. In fact, we need to be on a journey of discovery if we want to cultivate our ambition and accomplish our goals and desires. We have a God-given desire to seek out answers.

We were created to be fascinated and live a life of excitement searching out His endless depths. We were made in His image so we might be on the perpetual journey to be transformed into His likeness through the discovery of who He is and what He's like.

There is an adventure in searching that God wants to take us on, but what does this adventure look like? One does not go rummaging through a field, digging it up, hoping to find God. I decided to set myself on a journey to find out what it looks like to search out the depths of God's treasure.

Taking the Proverbs 2 approach to my Bible reading, I set myself to incline my ear and look eagerly for the treasures of God. I desperately needed to know Him. So I started by asking the Lord to show me what He's like and began looking for every description I could find that directly revealed something about Him—what He does, what He calls himself, and how and what He thinks. As I began filling up dozens of pages of writing, I realized that I really didn't know much about Him at all. I repeated this process and found that I was filling up new pages of descriptions I didn't see the first time.

As I read through the descriptions, I felt like I was staring right at Him. My heart came alive as I read them out loud. Truths about who He is hit me like waves of power crashing on my heart. I found myself coming back to it again and again when I was feeling down, discouraged, or needing some faith. Every time I'd read down the list I'd feel a shift take place. I had discovered unparalleled hidden treasure.

The more I learn about Him, the more I feel I don't know and need to search more. There is an endless mountain full of treasures in searching out the depths of God. We get to spend eternity mining its depths. It's a worthy and fulfilling life of adventure to search Him out. You were made for this. Set yourself on a journey to find out who He is. He will reveal Himself and you will be transformed.

Jesus, you are full of endless and fascinating treasures. Thank you for the invitation to spend our lives searching you out, and thank you that when we seek, we find, because you love to reveal yourself. Give me the grace to search deeper.

What would it look like for you to go on an adventure of discovering Him? What do you believe God wants to reveal to you? How can you make your ear attentive to hearing and incline your heart to understanding Him more?

SONG RECOMMENDATIONS

"As the Deer" by Matt Gilman and Jordan Sarmiento
from *Awaken Love*

"Who Is Like the Lord" by Christina Reynolds
from *Love Makes Us Strong*

DAY 35

Divine Authority

MATT GILMAN

Out of the mouth of babes and nursing infants
You have ordained strength,
Because of Your enemies,
That You may silence the enemy and the avenger.

PSALM 8:2

Every parent imagines meeting their child for the first time. It's a moment that will be remembered for the rest of their life. That first bonding moment filled with indescribable emotion and happiness, that first time you look into your child's eyes and say, "I love you," the first smile, the first diaper change ... OK, maybe the diaper change isn't that magical. But all in all, becoming a parent for the first time is an overwhelmingly joyous occasion.

So you can imagine the excitement I felt when I discovered I was about to be a father of twins. Double the excitement. Double the fear. Double the food. Double the diapers. It's a crazy emotion. I couldn't believe it.

Things didn't go exactly how I had planned, however. Due to a series of complications during pregnancy, my boys were born almost three months early. Immediately after delivery, they were rushed to the NICU, put on oxygen, had feeding tubes placed through their tiny nostrils and then were placed in an incubator.

I remember so vividly the emotions I felt when I was being escorted into their hospital room. I walked in and saw my son, Isaac, on the left side of the room, and my other son, Caden, on the right, each weighing just about three pounds apiece. I was already so proud of them. Proud that they were mine. But as I stayed longer, I wanted to hold them, just to touch them. But the layer of plexiglass remained between me and my sons.

In that moment, Psalm 8:2 came into my head. It had confused me before. But now, I knew that this verse couldn't be correct. Perhaps it was a typo in my Bible. Perhaps the actual words were lost in translation. But the statement "from the mouths of babes and infants you've ordained strength," made no sense to me. I was a brand-new parent, but even before the birth of my sons I recognized that babies couldn't do much of anything without help.

I began to accuse God. *How could you let this happen to me? How could you let this happen to them? This was not the way it was supposed to happen. How can that verse be true, Lord? Look at my sons. They would die if it weren't for these machines. They can't even breathe on their own!* I was so angry.

But even in my whirlwind of emotion, He answered me with such kindness—as if He could sympathize with me in the moment. His still, small voice spoke to me. Each phrase permeated with the revelation of His heart.

Oh, Matthew, don't you understand? Without me you can't breathe. Without me you can't move. I have ordained your every step. And it's in your weakness that my strength is made perfect.

Suddenly it made sense to me. It was never about what I can do on my own. It was always about partnership with Him. He could have designed creation any way He wanted to. He had a blank canvas. And He created *you*. Not so that you could run around and do His dirty work. Not because you could do something for Him that He couldn't already do Himself. He did not knit you together so intricately in your mother's womb because He needed you. He did it because He desired you. He created you for friendship. For partnership.

Your weakness doesn't surprise Him. He's never caught off guard by your failures or your sin. He's not leaning over the balcony of Heaven shaking His head in disappointment every time you stumble. He's overwhelmed that you said *yes* to this journey. And as you walk it out with humility and repentance, He is so faithful to command His lovingkindness over you. A love that covers a multitude of your sins.

And now that sin no longer has any power over you,

you are free to walk in your destiny. The rest of Psalm 8 goes on to say that He has crowned you with glory and honor. He has created you to have dominion over the works of His hand. He has put all things under your feet. As a human being, created in the image of God, you have been given governmental authority. When you pray in accordance with His will, things will always shift for the advancement of His kingdom.

You are royalty. You are chosen. You are loved. You are desired. And you have dominion granted to you by the authority of Heaven. Maybe you're confronted with your weakness in this season. But there is good news for you. We are all weak and broken. But it's in your weakness that His strength is made perfect. And it's in your frailty that His glory shines through. Partner with His heart today. It's what you were created for: partnership.

Father, reveal to me the authority that you've given me, and remind me that my weakness doesn't disqualify me from receiving your grace.

If you could actually see things shifting as you lifted up your voice in prayer, you would pray differently and more confidently. Pray today like you believe you have real authority. Declare the goodness of Jesus over each and every situation.

SONG RECOMMENDATIONS

"Standing in the Gap" by Tim Reimherr
from *Let the Weak Speak*

"Every Captive Free" by Matt Gilman
from *Awaken Love*

DAY 36

Kings and Priests

BRENTON DOWDY

To Him who loved us and washed us from our sins
in His own blood, and has made us kings and priests
to His God and Father, to Him be glory and dominion
forever and ever. Amen.

REVELATION 1:5B–6

I was a worship pastor at a megachurch in Texas when God told my little family to leave everything and follow Him. Abraham's story was becoming our reality. We sold our house, packed all of our stuff in a moving truck, and drove to Kansas City to be interns at the International House of Prayer—not knowing what or where would be next. When we got there, my internship assignments became leading worship for the four-year-old class, driving shuttles, and operating the lyric presenter in the prayer room. As valuable and precious as those roles are, my life had literally turned upside down. Sometimes I thought I was losing my mind. God had a lot to teach me about being a king, being a servant, and how upside-down heaven sees all of it.

We have been given a powerful and humbling privilege to partner with the Creator. We are broken and imperfect outside of the grace of Jesus, but He has called us to rule and reign with Him. Eventually, we are supposed to look like Him in glory. God is conforming us to be filled with grace and truth and to lead with confidence and authority as we follow in the footsteps of Christ. We are promised that we will reign *with* Him in glory.

All the way back to the garden we see the heart of God creating partnership with man. He created Adam, He fashioned Eve, and then He commissioned them to rule over what He created. As we know, things got a little messy, but God hasn't stopped the journey of redeeming this arrangement. Because of what Jesus accomplished in His resurrection, the redemption story is progressing perfectly. The Father is conforming us into the likeness of Jesus and steadily increasing our capacity to rule and reign the way He intends for it to be done. There are uncultivated territories, emotions, and cultures in you and around you that God intends for you to rule over and bring into alignment with His kingdom. If you're willing to see it from an eternal perspective, you won't miss it.

God is the ultimate ruler. He is the one that holds all things together. Everything was created by Him and for Him and continues to exist because of Him. However, the Being that is responsible for all of that is not only a ruler, but also a servant. Since we're created in His image, this twofold identity has been our destiny since the beginning. Not just *taking dominion*, but also *acting in service*.

Over and over again throughout Scripture we see the example of a life laid down. Life is more than merely being in control and feeling powerful. There is a significant piece missing if we do not understand that we were created to serve. We are called to lay down our lives for each other and to consider others more significant than ourselves. Priests serve. They serve God and they serve people. Being a priest was written into the beginning of our story at creation, and it is written into our future in Revelation. As servants, ministers, and ambassadors, we are called to represent Jesus to the world around us.

It's no coincidence that we're referred to as kings and priests in the same sentence. Each identity has to inform the other or we will end up in a mindset far from what God intended for us, regardless of which one we run after. Often, people try to rule from an arrogant and demanding place—it can be dangerous and even abusive. However, serving from a place of self-deprecation and a low sense of self-worth is equally incongruent with how Scripture says God feels about us. Our destiny is that we will walk in the fullness of both realities. What a gift from our Father! These concepts are not at war with each other. It is the presence of both mindsets that ensures we are living in God's intended design.

Jesus is the example of these realities lived out in perfection. He came as a man to serve, but He never stopped being a king. The one human that absolutely deserved to be served *instead* walked as a servant and gave up his life. He had nothing to prove to himself. The King of Heaven and Earth got down on His knees and washed filth off the feet of the ones He was leading. Everything we go through in this life is an opportunity to mature in how we *rule* and how we *serve*. It is all preparing us to reign with perfection in the age to come.

Father, I ask you to reveal to my heart where you're teaching me the ways of heavenly royalty and how I can align with what you're doing on the earth. Show me how to serve with the heart of a king and how to rule with the heart of a servant.

How is God calling you to mix both your identity as king and as priest? In what ways is He calling you to both rule and serve?

SONG RECOMMENDATIONS

"I Love the Way You Think"
by Misty Edwards (feat. Katie Reed)
from *Onething Live: All Cry Glory*

"Enthroned on Our Praises" by Brenton Dowdy
from *Love Makes Us Strong*

DAY 37

Strength to Persevere

JUSTIN RIZZO

He gives strength to the weary and increases the power of the weak. Even youths grow tired and weary, and young men stumble and fall; but those who hope in the Lord will renew their strength. They will soar on wings like eagles; they will run and not grow weary, they will walk and not be faint.

ISAIAH 40:29–31 (NIV)

Imagine that you're walking on a path leading up a magnificent mountain. The temperature is perfect and there's a nice breeze. You have your gear and you're making good time, each step bringing you closer to where the lush green grass melds into the snow-capped mountain peak.

In time, you come to a part of the path that's no longer paved but covered in muck and mud. Though it's hard to walk through, you press on because the mountain is majestic and you're on a mission.

But hours turn into days on this muddy section of path. You're barely moving. You look behind you and that same rock you passed yesterday is only a few feet back. You're tired and weary. That perfect day isn't perfect anymore. Flies begin buzzing around your head and your backpack seems so much heavier than before.

Frustration sets in.

You begin to ask yourself what happened to the smooth hiking.

As much as you may not want to hear it, this is a description of your life—all of our lives. We want an effortless ascent to the top of the mountain where everything is thriving—where work, family situations, and our lives in God are all established and flourishing. But the fact is that difficult and mundane parts of the journey leave you questioning whether you should press on or just give up and turn back.

In these places of testing, I hear God say, *My ultimate goal for you isn't that you get to the top of the mountain, but that you find me along the way. Let's talk to each other. Let's enjoy the journey together.*

Isaiah 40:29–31 tells us that in this life, we can expect to grow tired and weary and to stumble and fall. The seasons when it's slow going and we feel stuck in the mud often leave us weary and discouraged. But God's Word tells us that those who hope in the Lord will renew their strength. Notice that it doesn't say that there won't be any muck and mud, but that if we look to Him, He will give us the strength to push through it.

When the way before us is difficult, God's Word says that if we trust in Him with all of our strength, lean not on our own understanding, and acknowledge Him in all of our ways, He will make our paths straight (Prov. 3:5–6). The path might not be paved and easy, but He will lead us in the way we should go and be with us on the journey. In the seasons when you feel like you are merely surviving instead of thriving, God is yearning for you to reach out to Him and find joy in walking together.

In His kindness, God blesses us with joy, rest, and refreshment between and during the hard seasons. We tend to fixate on our current difficulty and forget the big picture. But God, who sees the end from the beginning, never loses sight of the plans that He has for us. Learn to stay in close conversation with Him and you will find that in those muddy times, He is there to give you hope (Jer. 29:11).

Lord, help me to know you in the messy seasons. Teach me to trust your leading when I feel like I'm just trudging through. Use the difficult times to show me you are with me and help me to delight in finding you there.

Write out Isaiah 40:29–31 and then write down areas you want the strength to persevere in.

SONG RECOMMENDATIONS:

"Strong in Grace" by Justin Rizzo from *Savior's Love*

"Come Now Joy" by Justin Rizzo from *Fully Alive*

DAY 38

His Voice
Gives Me Courage

LAUREN ALEXANDRIA DUECK

Arise, my dearest. Hurry, my darling.
Come away with me!
I have come as you have asked
to draw you to my heart and lead you out.
For now is the time, my beautiful one.

SONG OF SONGS 2:10B (TPT)

My face was splotchy and tear-stained, and my heart felt heavy. I needed some time alone, so I drove a couple miles down the road where no one would be. I think I cried every tear inside of me, and all I could say to God was *I need you, Abba, help me.* I was frustrated and afraid. Frustrated, because I couldn't control what was happening. My life seemed to be slipping through my fingers, and I was afraid because I had never seen or experienced a faith miracle before. I didn't know if God would *really* come through for me when I needed Him to. I waited for Him to speak. I was so completely real and vulnerable with Him in my mess of emotions.

Wow, He is so kind and patient! I imagined the Father gently putting His hands on my face and looking straight into my eyes. I felt His voice deep inside me say, *I'm with you.* And just like that, peace rushed over my mind and heart again, and I regained heaven's perspective. His voice gave me courage.

Song of Songs 2:10 says, "The one I love calls to me … Arise" (TPT). God doesn't promise that life will come without its challenges. In fact, the longer I live, the more I come to realize that He uses these mountains to cause our hearts to grow in love. Whereas before we had placed our comfort in our surroundings, He uses the hard things to draw us back to Himself. And this is the best place to be. Totally dependent on Him. Because as soon as we say *yes,* He rushes in, picks us up, and carries us right up that mountain. His words uphold us like mighty hands as His voice echoes *arise* through our being. There is just no other voice on Earth that can both challenge and empower us.

When I cried out to Him in the car that night, my confused little heart was saying, *Why is this happening to me? Why do I have to face this?* What I needed to know was that I wasn't alone. When life doesn't make sense, there is an opportunity to lean into His voice and commune with Him.

We were never meant to conquer the mountain on our own. He wants to give us power in our weakness, love in our brokenness, and a sound mind free from our anxieties. He wants to deliver us from fear through His love, ruling and reigning over our hearts at each step of the journey. Something that feels impossible at first will either cause us to withdrawl in fear or come away with Him and conquer the mountain of fear together.

The discomfort of trials and change creates dependency on Him, and the more we lean into Him, the larger our faith for the impossible begins to grow. Our hearts become intertwined with His as our history goes deep. And before we know it, we are standing right on top of that mountain as overcomers—victorious ones because He is with us, having carried us all the way.

Father, help me face the mountain in front of me. It's hard, but you're bigger. Give me strength in my weakness, uphold me with your words, and keep me near, leaning on you.

What are some challenges in your life that are keeping you from fully trusting the Father's leadership? How can you take those areas of fear and turn them into prayers of surrender?

SONG RECOMMENDATIONS

"Victorious in Love" by Lauren Alexandria
from *Victorious in Love*

"Still Looking Back at Me" by Jon Thurlow
from *Different Story*

DAY 39

The Nations Are Singing Together

JIM STERN

And they sang a new song with these words:
"You are worthy to take the scroll
and break its seals and open it.
For you were slaughtered,
and your blood has ransomed people for God
from every tribe and language and people and nation.
And you have caused them to become
a Kingdom of priests for our God.
And they will reign on the earth."

REVELATION 5:9–10 (NLT)

If anyone was a part of a local church in the United States during the 1970s and '80s, you can testify to the fact that there were many changes taking place in the worship culture of the body of Christ. For those of you who weren't there, or who weren't alive yet, please envision ...

Mauve-colored carpet because it was the official carpet color of almost every auditorium in the country.

Worship teams and the volunteer audio guy at church embraced a rainbow of colors on the stage. New lighting? No, it was a collection of the largest foam microphone covers that the world had ever seen. Arguments about contemporary worship were alive and well also. Do contemporary-sounding worship songs still count as worship? Can we play drums in church or are drums associated with voodoo rhythms in Africa? If we use some distortion on our electric guitars, will Jesus be praised or will we be on the stairway to heaven Led Zeppelin is on?

Little did anyone in the early '80s know that just a few years later, by the year 2000, the youth movements from almost every part of the body of Christ, in almost every nation of the earth, were singing the same worship songs and responding to Jesus in worship in very similar ways. Think of it like this: the expression of corporate worship in the majority of the nations was transformed in just one generation! And now it is normal to have global songs being sung to Jesus and, because of technology, even global worship leaders directing hearts to join with the realities of worship in heaven.

In Revelation 5, we are brought into a dynamic and prophetic moment where all of heaven is captivated and fascinated by the worth and value of Jesus' leadership. There was a conclusion that the angels and the elders of old have come to, and it is threefold:

- Jesus gave His life for every people group across the earth.

- He has made the saints from every nation to be priests before God, clothed in His righteousness, and given a position of authority as a co-heir with Him.

- Jesus is the only one qualified to have the unlimited resources of the nations at His disposal and handle them in a righteous way.

With anyone else, "absolute power corrupts absolutely," but not with Jesus. And because of this truth, heaven is enamored. This same captivation with Jesus' leadership is happening in the global Church today and we sing His name, grow in our priestly identity, and unite in spirit with our spiritual family around the world. God is maturing His people in every nation as we continue to sing, "You are worthy!"

With that being said, we must consider that during these years God's Spirit is arranging and rearranging the worship of Jesus in every nation to create a global symphony that unites with the continuous worship that is in heaven. For the singers and musicians that are active in the daily and weekly effort of making corporate worship happen, there will be great persistence required and progress will often feel slow. But when we lift our eyes up to the global picture, the evidence is undeniable ... the worship of God in the nations is being transformed on our watch. It's an incredible time to be alive.

God, thank you for your leadership and for the global songs that you are raising up. I am privileged to be invited into the transformation of worship in the nations. Father, I ask that in every tribe, tongue, people, and language there would be songs of love and proclamations of your goodness being released as earth and heaven become incrementally united.

Think about how you have seen worship in your personal life and in corporate experiences grow and change during your time as a worshiper of Jesus. Write down the areas where you've seen growth and progress. Take a few moments to meditate on Revelation 5:9–10. Ask the Father for a greater revelation of the worth and value of His Son and write down the aspects of Christ's worth that are revealed to your heart.

SONG RECOMMENDATIONS:

"From the Ends of the Earth" by Ryan Kondo
from *Onething Live: Sing Your Praises*

"There Is One Found Worthy" by Justin Rizzo
from *Onething Live: Magnificent Obsession*

DAY 40

Your Shepherd
Is a Dreamer

ANNA BLANC

The Lord is my shepherd; I shall not want.

PSALM 23:1

I did *not* want to marry Chris MacDonald. But he loved
Jesus and wanted to be a missionary. So God was
going to make me marry him, right? My seventh-grade
thinking is laughable now, but if I'm honest, it's a pattern
I've wrestled with for years. In high school I loved music
and loved to sing. I figured God would want me to lay
that on the altar and be done with it.

Want to have a family? Better lay that down.
Reaching for success in business or impact in ministry? I
won't get my hopes up.

I am guilty of imagining that God's best for me is
to step into a proverbial prison cell. If I have a desire for
something, then that must mean I am not to have it. Or
possibly worse: if I didn't want something, it was bound
to be God's will for my life.

I think the best weapon the enemy has is to twist our understanding of who God is. If he can lead us to believe that God is hard to please—a taskmaster who enjoys inflicting boredom and want on the obedient— then Satan is guaranteed the safety of impotent believers who stand at a distance, easily pacified. It takes no effort on his part. We step willingly into our prison cells, allowing the passion within to die away.

But what if we have it all wrong?

What if God is the very one shouting loudly from the mountaintops, calling any who will hear to the heights of adventure? "Come out! Come away with me" (Song. 2:10)! What if we are standing neatly in our cells with chains around our wrists that aren't even locked?

Many believers are familiar with the promises of Psalm 23: "The Lord is my shepherd, I shall not want." Beautiful words filled with promise and life. Yet, I'm guilty of boiling it down to insipid poetry. Words.

But do you hear the promise ringing out into the hollows of the prison cells from the tops of the mountains? *You shall not want.*

You, twenty-year-old young man made for the outdoors with a heart that comes alive as you rock climb. You've scaled most of the 14ers in Colorado! And now you're following Jesus. *Wait.* Don't walk numbly toward that cell just yet. Can you hear Him calling from the peaks you've yet to climb? You shall not want for adventure.

I see you too, thirty-six-year-old mother of three.

With the dried snot wiped on your thigh and the macaroni burning on the stove. Maybe you feel like you're already in that locked room some days. But I know the furtive glances you've cast at the kitchen junk drawer that hold your brushes—tools that have painted sunsets and seed pods and brilliantly colored abstracts. What if the stirring in your soul to take a chance on canvas again is not discontent with your season. What if that is the call of the Shepherd? You shall not want for adventure.

Calling all travelers, all poets, all accountants, and dads. Nurses, pilots, and mathematicians. You shall not want for adventure.

The Shepherd of our souls—the very author of this life story—is standing on the cliff's edge, calling. There's nothing about your well-manicured existence in prison that excites Him. He imagined the billions of stars glaring out from galaxies yet undiscovered. And now you're going to honor Him by crouching in the corner, hands over your eyes, safely waiting out the years?

Your Shepherd is a dreamer.

Maybe the best way to honor Him is to dare to dream again. You shall not want for adventure.

Jesus, help me to see and experience you as the one who made me with a longing for adventure. Stir my heart to dream big dreams with you again.

What is one previously abandoned dream that you feel the Holy Spirit inviting you to pick back up again?

SONG RECOMMENDATIONS

"Torches" by Lauren Alexandria Dueck
from *Fully Alive*

"Heart Celebration" by Laura Hackett Park
from *Fully Alive*

About the Authors

JUSTIN RIZZO was born and raised in Buffalo, New York, where he developed a passion and love for music at an early age. He began playing a variety of instruments and started leading worship at age twelve. He has released five albums and been featured on multiple compilation projects along with writing and producing two full-length musicals. In addition, he travels extensively to lead worship and speak at conferences and events around the world. Justin is currently a full-time staff member at IHOPKC. Connect with Justin at justinrizzo.com.

LAURA HACKETT PARK has been a worship leader and prophetic singer at IHOPKC since 2000. From the beginning days of this ministry, Laura felt called to join and minister to the Lord with prayer, worship, and music. After five years at the University of Missouri-Kansas City, she earned a Bachelor of Music Theory at their conservatory. She has since devoted herself to songwriting, Bible study, and leading worship at IHOPKC. Laura is married to fellow worship leader and songwriter, Jonas Park, and they have two children. Connect with Laura at laurahackettpark.com.

JON THURLOW is a worship leader, song writer, and intercessor at IHOPKC. He grew up in a musical environment and cultivated a love for music at an early age. Jon studied classical piano from age eight to twenty-two and holds a bachelor's degree in sacred music. Jon has been married to the love of his life, Kinsey, for the better part of a decade and is father to Autumn. Connect with Jon at jonthurlow.com.

MATT GILMAN has been leading worship since he was fourteen years old. After graduating high school, Matt moved to Kansas City where he served for ten years as a worship leader in the IHOPKC prayer room. Matt served at the Orlando House of Prayer for five years. He currently travels with a collective of worship artists called Influence Music. Matt resides in Orlando, Florida, with his wife, Kelly, and his twin boys, Isaac and Caden. Connect with Matt on Facebook, Twitter, and Instagram @gilmanmatt.

JOSHUA ALDY grew up in Mississippi as a worship leader at his church and local house of prayer. Since 2011, he has lived in Kansas City where he serves full-time at IHOPKC. He's had the privilege of playing in front of gatherings of up to 30,000 people and traveling with different IHOPKC artists. He is passionate about writing and creating music to glorify Jesus. Additionally, he and his wife, Emily, teach and disciple children from all over the world through weekly Bible classes. They have three children of their own. Connect with Joshua at joshuaaldy.com.

In 2004 CALEB ANDREWS moved from Houston, Texas, to IHOPKC for an internship. After a year in Kansas City, he moved to Atlanta to help start a house of prayer. He currently lives in Atlanta with his wife and six kids and serves full-time as a worship leader at the International House of Prayer in Atlanta. Connect with Caleb at ihop-atlanta.com.

Growing up in a God-fearing home, ROBBY ATWOOD received Jesus as his Lord and Savior at an early age. At seventeen, he had an encounter with the Holy Spirit that would forever change the course of his life. With this encounter came a renewed focus to pursue the Lord and the ministry he had been called to. For nearly twelve years, he faithfully served at a prominent local church as a worship and prayer leader. In 2006, Robby received a clear word to build the house of prayer. Robby now directs One27 House of Prayer in Somerset, Kentucky. Robby resides in Somerset with his beautiful wife, Misty, and their two children, Luke and Olivia. Connect with Robby at robbyatwood.com.

MICHAEL and BECCI BALL are worship leaders, songwriters, and directors of Manchester House of Prayer in the UK. They have a desire to see people awakened to the worth of Jesus and to connect people to the heart of God. They have been married since 2004 and have four phenomenal children. Connect with Michael and Becci at michaelandbecciball.com.

ANNA BLANC has been a singer and worship leader at IHOPKC since 2005. Anna has written a book called *Growing as a Prophetic Singer* and has taught an advanced class on prophetic singing at the music school at International House of Prayer University. Anna lives with her husband, Shawn, and their three sons in Kansas City, Missouri. Connect with Anna at theblancspot.com.

Originally from Abilene, Texas, BRENTON DOWDY has been serving at IHOPKC with his wife, Cara, and their three children since 2014. They currently lead a worship team at the prayer room and lead services at Forerunner Church. Connect with Brenton at brentondowdy.com.

KENDRIAN DUECK is a part-time worship leader with IHOPKC and the worship leader for Journey Church International in Kansas City. Born in Winnipeg, Canada, into a small, tight-knit church community, singing and worshiping has always been a passion. He and his wife, Lauren (Alexandria Dueck), reside in Lee's Summit where they continue to serve both the prayer movement and the local church. Connect with Kendrian at laurenandkendrian.com.

LAUREN ALEXANDRIA DUECK is a full-time intercessory missionary and worship leader at the International House of Prayer in Kansas City where she and her husband, Kendrian, live. She grew up in Phoenix, Arizona, and moved to Kansas City in 2012. She attended IHOPU for four years as a Forerunner Music Academy student before officially joining staff. Her life's mission is to see a generation of passionate, burning lovers of God be raised up to proclaim the worth of Jesus and His great return. Connect with Lauren at laurenandkendrian.com.

CALEB EDWARDS is a worship leader, preacher, teacher, and leader at IHOPKC. He and his wife, Kaila, live in Kansas City with their two children. They share a collective vision to strengthen the church's love for Jesus and advance day and night worship and prayer. Connect with Caleb at calebedwards.org.

LISA GOTTSHALL grew up in Pennsylvania in a large family with an Amish background. She moved to Kansas City in 1998 for Bible school and has been involved with IHOPKC since 1999 as a singer, worship leader, and teacher. She and her husband, John, have two children, Abigail and Andrew. Lisa's passion is to experience and share with others the extravagant love of Jesus. She loves taking part in the "singing seminary," learning the Word through singing it. Connect with Lisa at lisagottshall.bandcamp.com.

JOHAN HEINRICHS serves on staff as an intercessory missionary at Sanctuary House of Prayer in Winnipeg, Manitoba, where he lives with his wife, Corrie, and three children, Eli, Caitlin, and Luke. In addition to his ministry as an intercessory missionary, he is a worship leader and songwriter. He has also authored the book *Audience of One: Discovering Ministry to God* and co-authored *Let Us Pray: A Manual for Strengthening Corporate Prayer in Your Region*. Connect with Johan at johanheinrichs.com.

VERONIKA and SEBASTIAN LOHMER are both leaders who serve full time at the house of prayer in Augsburg, Germany. They have two sons, Immanuel and Elia, and love traveling and leading people into the presence of God. Connect with Veronika and Sebastian at gebetshaus.org.

Raised in Tallahassee, Florida, BRANDON OAKS has sung and played guitar since 2003. He is a singer, producer, and sound engineer, and plays electric guitar, drums, and bass. Playing primarily electric since 2011, he has led worship at IHOPKC since 2014. He is married to Morgan. Brandon has a passion to write songs, lead worship, and train musicians how to both grow in their skills and cultivate a spirit of prophecy and intercession. Connect with Brandon at brandonoaks.wordpress.com.

NAOMI RIZZO was born and raised in Tallahassee, Florida, where she developed a love for singing through worship. After spending time in Israel, she attended Lee University where she studied theology and voice before joining the full-time staff at IHOPKC. For twelve years she's served as a singer and worship leader, and has taught voice classes at IHOPKC. She resides in Kansas City with her husband, Justin, and two children. Connect with Naomi on Twitter and Instagram @rizzettenaomi.

EMILAINE SOUSA is part of the senior leadership of the Florianopolis House of Prayer (FHOP), a local church and missions organization based on a vision to combine 24/7 prayer with worship. She takes leadership over the prayer room as well as takes the role of a worship leader and songwriter. Emi is married to Vinicius Sousa. They both grew up in London, helped start the house of prayer in London (IHOP-London), and later on moved to Kansas City and graduated from International House of Prayer University. They now live in Florianopolis, Brazil. Connect with Emilaine on Facebook at emilaine.assis and Instagram @emilaine_sousa.

JIM STERN has been the lead pastor at Destiny Church in St. Louis since 2006 and has a background in music and worship in the local church. Jim and his wife, Jessica, are the proud and slightly overwhelmed parents of four beautiful daughters and one son. Connect with Jim at jimstern.org.

JAYE THOMAS is a Dove Award-nominated singer/ songwriter and has been leading worship since 1993. He has written and recorded with many artists and has traveled extensively around the world, teaching and training worship leaders and teams on songwriting, team dynamics, and prophetic singing. He is the director of the Forerunner School of Worship within the International House of Prayer University and worship leader at Connection Pointe Church. Jaye and his wife, Nayomi, have three beautiful children and live in Kansas City, Missouri. Connect with Jaye at jayethomas.com.

LUKE WOOD has been a worship leader and songwriter since 2003. He served on the leadership team at IHOPKC from 2004–2014. Luke, his wife, Leah, and their three children currently live in Colorado Springs. Connect with Luke at lukewoodmusic.co.

Take the prayer room anywhere...free.

JOIN US LIVE 24/7

ONLINE
Vist ihopkc.org

SMART TV
Available on Roku

MOBILE APP
Available on
iPhone and Android

ihopkc.org/prayerroom

24/7 LIVE WORSHIP & PRAYER SINCE 1999

International House *of* Prayer
MISSIONS BASE OF KANSAS CITY

On September 19, 1999, a prayer meeting began that continues to this day; from dawn to dusk and through the watches of the night, by the grace of God, prayer and worship have continued twenty-four hours a day, seven days a week.

Learn more at ihopkc.org/about